Iridescent Grace

The Journey from Pain to Pearls

Carly Richaven

Copyright © 2016 Carly Richaven.

All rights reserved. No part of this book may be used or reproduced by any means, graphic, electronic, or mechanical, including photocopying, recording, taping or by any information storage retrieval system without the written permission of the author except in the case of brief quotations embodied in critical articles and reviews.

This book is a work of non-fiction. Unless otherwise noted, the author and the publisher make no explicit guarantees as to the accuracy of the information contained in this book and in some cases, names of people and places have been altered to protect their privacy.

Scripture taken from the King James Version of the Bible.

WestBow Press books may be ordered through booksellers or by contacting:

WestBow Press
A Division of Thomas Nelson & Zondervan
1663 Liberty Drive
Bloomington, IN 47403
www.westbowpress.com
1 (866) 928-1240

Because of the dynamic nature of the Internet, any web addresses or links contained in this book may have changed since publication and may no longer be valid. The views expressed in this work are solely those of the author and do not necessarily reflect the views of the publisher, and the publisher hereby disclaims any responsibility for them.

Any people depicted in stock imagery provided by Thinkstock are models, and such images are being used for illustrative purposes only.
Certain stock imagery © Thinkstock.

ISBN: 978-1-5127-3778-3 (sc)
ISBN: 978-1-5127-3779-0 (hc)
ISBN: 978-1-5127-3777-6 (e)

Library of Congress Control Number: 2016906616

Print information available on the last page.

WestBow Press rev. date: 04/22/2016

To those who hurt or struggle with fear, may you find perfect peace.

Foreword

Within these pages, Carly Richaven takes us on a journey that gives us hope in the midst of pain and tragedy. Very seldom can an author let you experience the weight of such heartache and, at the same time, inspire you with hope to overcome. Carly invites you to read her story, to experience the tragedy and, more important, the truth of God's redemptive power as He rescues her. Her story will captivate you and draw you in. Once you begin reading this book, you'll find it hard to put down.

During my eighteen years of full-time ministry, there have been a few times when someone's story is so disturbing that I knew only God could be responsible for his or her sanity. But sanity in itself is not the end road. Carly helps us see that Jesus came to give us life with abundance. That abundance includes grace, mercy, forgiveness, and perfect peace. I praise God that she allowed the Holy Spirit to heal her so that others may benefit from her experience.

My prayer is that this book will be the catalyst to help others find that same healing that only comes through Jesus Christ. May your pain transform into pearls in the presence of a Father who loves you right where you are.

—Bishop R. Thomas

Bishop Thomas is ordained with the Church of God, headquartered in Cleveland, Tennessee.

Preface

This story was written a few years ago, lifted from the pages of my personal journal. I wrote in my journal during several years of Christian counseling with a mental health therapist. My journaling helped me to understand and organize my thoughts at a time when I felt very overwhelmed. I needed to get the words out of me and onto paper so that I could move forward.

More than that, I wrote the story because I wanted to put all the pieces together, facts followed by meaning, into a flowing account of my life that I could comprehend. I organized the pieces and put the puzzle together to make a picture. Some pieces are dark, others are colorful, and still others, bright white. Isn't that true of almost every puzzle? And once it is done, there is nothing puzzling about it. The picture is clear.

Also, after having recorded the truth, I could walk away from it. If I ever needed to, I could reread the story and remember the lessons of truth God taught me. Those are the most important parts of my story: the lessons learned from Him. People who knew me marveled at the change in me. They said I went from trudging through the mud of life day by day to walking as light as a feather, three feet off the ground. Indeed, life had taken on new meaning and absolute joy.

Once it was all on paper, I talked about it to a few close friends who urged publication, but nothing seemed to work out at the time. So I put the whole thing on the shelf, brushed my hands, and thought I was through with it.

When it was suggested again that I publish my story to help others who had experienced similar pain, I considered it and then let the ugliness of the abuse convince me not to publish. Sometime later, a friend told me of a writing contest she'd seen advertised and thought of me. At her urging, I sent it in, but when it didn't win and get published through that avenue, I was glad. I was sure then that leaving it on the shelf was the best idea. People who didn't know me before but knew me at this point had no idea of the troubles I'd seen. I wanted it that way. It was my shot at being normal. Pathetic, I know.

Others close to me continued to ask about the book, encouraging me to publish, to which I replied, "When the time is right." Secretly, I meant twenty or more years—or how about never? I let a few folks read the manuscript when they asked, even though I felt they would consider me a lunatic. *One more friendship down the drain*, I thought. When would I learn? Much to my surprise, they did not think I was crazy and again encouraged publication. I planned to let it stay on the shelf.

It has been my experience—and probably yours too—that our plans and God's plans are often at odds. A short time ago, I felt the nudging of the Holy Spirit to take the book off the shelf. I have seen firsthand that His plans are perfect, while mine are rather selfish. He reminded me that it was not just my story, but our story, and He wanted others to experience the peace I had. I know this peace only because of God, and I never, ever say no to Him, so I handed the book to Him, giving Him total control over it. After some editing and adding some incidents He inspired me to include, I sent it for publication.

It is my heartfelt desire that you sense God's grace and glory in this book more than you feel my pain. And as you read it, I hope you open the door and invite Him into your story.

Acknowledgments

To our heavenly Father, I bow before You. My love for You is exceeded only by Your love for me, as evidenced in the pages of this book. I pray others will come to know more of Your true nature as they walk this journey with us.

To Jesus, Lord of all I am and all I have, there are no words to adequately express what You mean to me. Without You, this would just be another sad story of abused children.

To Paul, God's servant and my friend, thank you for lending your expertise to Jesus and me.

To my husband of forty-three years, whose unfailing love and support throughout our marriage cannot be compared, I love you so much.

To Macie, my daughter and best friend, your gentle heart for people who are hurting is amazing.

To Rob, my only son, I love you beyond words. You are your daddy and me meshed together: my sense of humor, his awesomeness.

To Anna, my daughter and best friend, your quiet strength calms the crazy.

To Lori, my sister and BFF, I love you more.

To Wendy, my sister and BFF, you still make me smile.

To April and Jake, thank you for loving and trusting me.

To Dean, I love you and pray for you often.

To Brent and Glenda, thank you for those late-night chats. What a comfort you are.

To Vickie, best friend, there for each other we always will be.

To my pastor, thank you for seeing me through some tough stuff and for keeping me grounded. You are wise beyond your years. And to my pastor's wife, your sweet spirit gives me strength. Thank you for encouraging me.

To all of my church family, thank you for hurting with me, growing with me, and laughing with me. The best is yet to come.

To my support group—my extended family and friends, too many to name—thank you for all of the hours (years) you spent listening, trying to understand, consoling, and loving me. The encouragement you gave enabled me to give it to God, move forward, and get it done.

Author's Note: This is a memoir. The memories are mine, corroborated by my siblings, other eyewitnesses, medical evidence, and military records. All of the names have been changed and any identifiable information removed to protect both the innocent and the guilty. This story is not about the abused or the abusers. It is about the Savior and His amazing grace. The goal in publishing this book is to reveal the true nature of God, His mercy, and His love, in the hope that others may find the peace I have found.

The Lord is my light and my salvation.
—Psalm 27:1

1

Sitting cross-legged on the right side of our dark-cherry sleigh bed, I peered into my husband's open nightstand drawer. My eyes were fixed on the .22-caliber pistol nestled among the contents, the cold, gunmetal gray a mirror image of my soul. Deep inside me, the last fiber of good sense battled an overwhelming desire to be dead. I didn't necessarily want to kill myself; I just wanted to *be* dead. Nightmares interrupted my sleep almost every night. Fear and anxiety were my constant companions.

I used to enjoy lounging around on Saturday mornings but not anymore. Even the silky feel of my pajamas did nothing to lift my mood. My husband, Grant, up at six with airboat in tow by seven, was fishing on the Gulf and wouldn't be back until after dark. Our youngest daughter, Anna, slept in her one-bedroom apartment attached to the other side of our house and wouldn't stir until noon. I had about an hour left.

The Florida sun streamed slivers of light into the room through long, thin gaps in the curtains at each window. Moments before, I had been standing at one of the large nine-paned bedroom windows, slightly parting the curtains to investigate a commotion. Two redbirds squabbled at the bird feeder, disrupting for a moment the usual quiet of our backyard. As one flew away, the other began to sing, inciting others to join in.

It wasn't long ago the deadness of winter had yielded to spring. Gardenia and rose buds burst forth and matured, perfuming their surroundings, while cardinals, blue jays, and even the plain brown mockingbirds performed like there was something to sing about. I could see it and hear it; I just couldn't feel it. Evidence of life was everywhere—except in me.

"Shut up, birds." I put my hands to my ears. *Silence. Better.* The winter's bleakness, long gone for most, clung to me. *Why am I like this?* I longed to know. My mind ran through the gamut of concerns, searching for anything that would shed light on the root cause of my incessant apprehension.

My husband was wonderful. Our three children were grown and doing well. We'd had a difficult time with our youngest daughter—crack cocaine and the lifestyle that went with it—but counseling had turned her around. *Could her past struggle be haunting me?*

Our oldest daughter, Macie, soon to graduate from college with a degree in computer science, had called yesterday. *No problems there.* Rob, our son, had a good job and a fine family, though he'd had his rough times. *Haven't we all?*

A wave of panic smothered me. *Why now?* My chest tightened. My fingers began tingling. *Lord, help me.* I wanted to scream but knew if I did, then I would never stop. Forcing myself to take slow, deep breaths, I looked around for something to refocus on—anything that would keep my mind tuned to the present.

On the floor by the dresser, a mountain of clothes waited to be washed, dried, and put away. *All that laundry for just two people?* Focusing on that, I calculated there were about six loads. I took another deep breath and continued to look around the room.

The huge dark-cherry dresser, cluttered and layered in dust, stood as a testament to my increased apathy to housecleaning. The tall bulky chest of drawers on the opposite wall wore the dust-covered silk plant like the headpiece of a shroud. Even the "Footprints" wall hanging, coated in dust, drooped. Heaviness surrounded me. *This place looks like a mausoleum. Perfect.*

I squared myself on the bed. The subtle Florida coastal theme I'd used to decorate this room originally had diminished the impact of the massive furniture. The king-sized comforter—a seashore print of soft aqua dotted with shells of antique gold, burgundy, and turquoise—once had brightened the room. Now, in spite of the slender surges of sunlight pouring in, the room was dark, depressing, and dusty.

Everywhere I looked, something needed to be cleaned, washed, or put up. *I'm through—through with all of it. My arms weigh a ton, and my legs have no strength. Even my head feels heavy. It's just too much. I don't even want to think anymore. I am tired of pushing myself. Dead is ... dead. No thinking, no pressure. Only dark, silence, and then peace.*

I heard my phone *ding* in my purse. A new text. *Don't care. Too tired.*

I noticed my black leather school bag leaning against the wall and remembered the papers I needed to grade. *Great. Something else that needs to be done. I'd forgotten about them.*

I swallowed. My throat was dry. *Paperwork, lesson plans, test scores. Stress. Is that what's overpowered me, placing this dark hood over my head?* No. At school, the fear faded into the background, and mounds of paperwork had never bothered me, not even during the months I graded essays. *Essays. Ugh.* I hated grading them. At least the state test was over, and I wasn't letting the kids down. It was May, the end of the school year. *Yeah, the kids are ready for that.*

Of the kids—130 of someone else's hormone-riddled fourteen-year-olds—a few would be sad. None would understand. Someone would counsel them. I'm just a teacher; they'd get over it. My coworkers would sit together on a pew at the funeral, shake their heads, and say they had no idea.

True. They have no idea. Who will find me? I don't care. Who will clean up this place? Don't care. At least I won't have to do it. I am tired of cleaning and cooking. I'm tired of everything. There is always too much to do. Mother's Day is coming up. I'm supposed to pick up tiger lilies for Grant's mom. He'll have to do it this year. And he can order Mama some irises; they're her favorite.

My chest hurt; I felt hollow. *Maybe I need to eat something. What's the point? People eat to live. I don't want to live. I'm tired.* I lay back on the pillow and longed to melt into the bed. My eyes closed.

Sinking farther into the abyss, I pictured my demise. *Pills wouldn't be as messy, but if they find me too soon and revive me, I'd have to do it all over again. At least with a pistol ...*

The calm voice of a friend broke into my thoughts. "*You know, you do have a choice. You can choose death, or you can choose to live.*"

Recognizing the voice, I looked up and saw a small circle of light. I spoke to the light. "Living is heavy. It makes me tired. I don't want to do it anymore."

I knew Jesus cared, but the choice was still mine. I had been a Christian for many years and knew the choice I was supposed to make. I also knew the consequences, but I was just too tired to fight anymore.

As the circle of light came closer, I saw my strong, faithful friend step into the fray, point a sword in the direction of the enemy I couldn't see, and turn His face to me. The hope in His eyes penetrated my soul. "What do you choose?" He asked softly but firmly, as if everything depended on my answer.

I felt strength in His voice, a surety that, given the right, He would fight for me—and win. Clinging to that strength—not mine but His—I decided, "Life. I choose life."

The scene faded as the light became bigger and brighter, and the tightness in my chest eased. I felt a peace in the room. From the light, Jesus said, "Let Me help you climb out of that hole."

As I looked around, I saw dark, moss-covered stones inside an old, deep, dry well. How did I get here? Taking a breath, I nodded and raised my hands to Him.

When I opened my eyes again, I worried that the light and the small window of peace I so needed would disappear. It didn't. I stood and leaned against the bed, my outer self fully functioning but my inner self clear in my mind. Deep inside, I saw the dark, dry well with a much younger me inside, staring up. Weird.[1]

A part of me still wanted to be dead, but another part decided to give Jesus a chance. I convinced myself He could correct the flaws in my thinking and end the nightmares and daytime terrors. He could give me peace, if anyone could. He was my last, best hope.

Of one thing I was certain, I could not and would not continue to barely grip sanity on a day-by-day basis. My way or His way, there would be a change.

Deciding to take one step at a time, I closed the nightstand drawer, reserving the right to open it again if His plan didn't work out.

I knew the next step: set up an appointment with Paul Thompson, the only counselor I knew and trusted. Since Anna had an appointment scheduled with him in three days, I decided to wait and make the appointment in person, rather than by phone. I felt more comfortable with the thought of discussing my present state of mind privately in the counselor's office than have it bouncing from cell tower to cell tower.

Sitting on the floor, I began to sort the laundry. Ignoring the dust and clutter everywhere, I focused for the moment only on gathering my husband's work clothes and getting them clean by Monday. Like a robot, I went through the motions, my mind wandering back many months.

Paul Thompson, a Christian counselor and licensed mental health professional, had been Anna's therapist for about ten months. Originally, when she came to stay with us to get her life back on track, Grant and I decided counseling was a must. Drugs and a life on the street had taken a toll on her mental stability. My heart broke to think of the times our grown child had been beaten or otherwise abused. With no job, I could only imagine what she had to go through to get the drugs her body craved. I didn't even want to know. As glad as we were to have her back under our roof where we knew she was safe, we weren't comfortable with her mental state.

At the time, I didn't know a good Christian counselor, but I remembered that my sister Lori did. I called her, and she helped us get the first appointment, beginning Anna's trek back to a purposeful life.

Lori first met Paul at the church they both attended. When depression and anxiety became unbearable in her life, she made an appointment with him and found peace. She urged me on several occasions to see Paul, since he had helped her. "Just one appointment and you will see," she said. I thought I handled my problems fine on my own. I had neither the time nor the need for counseling. I was wrong.

On Monday I went to work, no one the wiser about my unfinished Saturday project. Later, I told Anna I wanted to go to Paul's office with her the next day. To my relief, she agreed and didn't ask why.

On Tuesday, I lounged in the counselors' waiting room, grading papers until my eyes almost crossed and then flipping through the pages of a book I'd brought—anything to pass the time until the end of Anna's session. If I was going to do this, I wanted to get on with it. I am a get-it-done kind of person.

When Anna finished and headed to the restroom, I mentioned to Paul some of the dark thoughts I had been having. Concerned, he talked with me then. When Anna scheduled her next counseling appointment, I also set up one of my own with him.

Little did I realize this would begin an incredible, life-changing journey.

2

As I slipped out of bed before dawn on the day of my first counseling appointment, a picture flashed across my mind: several bowling balls rolled slowly right to left. *Hmmm, okay.*

Running my bath water, I wondered what the scene meant. It's not unusual for pictures to flash across my mind. A visual learner, I discover and retain information best by seeing it. What I hear also plays a part in my gathering and understanding of knowledge but not as much as what I see. As a young student, when I tried to understand something new, my teacher employed symbolism to create a link between what I already knew and the new information—a strategy that has always worked well for me.

As I relaxed in the bath, the scene unfolded again. Each of the black bowling balls had a short length of chain attached. Some were joined together by these chains. Two of the balls increased in speed and changed into black balloons, which floated upward, the chains becoming black ribbons. After floating upward about six to eight feet, they burst.

Interesting. Did I dream that? I shrugged it off, toweled dry, and got ready for work.

Later that day, I hurried home to pick up Anna for our appointments with the counselor, her twentieth or so and my first, and we started the two-hour trip to Paul's office. Recently, more often than not, Anna had been driving herself to her appointments in my car, a late-model Toyota Avalon with comfy interior and great sound system.

When she first started going to therapy, I drove her, literally and figuratively, because she fought us on the whole "counseling thing." She didn't think she needed that kind of counseling; a few meetings with Narcotics Anonymous, and she would be fine, she said. After several visits to Paul Thompson Counseling, however, she admitted he helped her.

Anna has never been much of a talker, so before we'd even leave the driveway for those initial visits, she'd settle back, close her eyes, and plug her earphones into the music of Journey. This trip would be no different. She rested comfortably in the front passenger seat, eyes closed and earphones in place, as I sped down the highway, lost in my own thoughts, accompanied by smooth jazz.

I was torn. Part of me wanted to get to the bottom of whatever felt so heavy; the other part wanted it to stay buried. The part that wanted to get better pushed me on. I remembered the light and felt strengthened. He said He would help me climb out. *Well, Lord, I sure need Your help today.*

I'm not sure when Jesus first became a part of my life. As a child, I went down to the front near the altar benches in a little Baptist church in southern Georgia one Sunday morning when the preacher gave the invitation. Aunt Rose looked my way and smiled her I'll-go-with-you-if-you-want-me-to smile. I didn't really understand the whole idea of inviting Jesus into my life, but I'd do anything to please Aunt Rose. To me, if sugar had a name, it would be hers. When Dean, my older brother, and I got to the front, the altar workers whisked us off into a small room where we knelt and prayed the Sinner's Prayer. It felt like we were making a promise and joining a club. Then they whisked us back out front and introduced us as "new creatures." People clapped. Obviously, our decision meant something special to the people in the church.

I got emotional because I'd made so many people happy. It wasn't something I normally did. Usually, I caused adults to get angry, particularly Mama. I was glad she hadn't come with us. I knew she probably would have frowned upon us joining this club.

Basking in the obvious approval of the crowd, I swelled with emotion. The church folks, including Aunt Rose, thought my tears fell because Jesus had done a work in my life. He had, but I didn't realize the scope of it until many years later.

When Aunt Rose later told Mama about the church service, she was upset with Mama for not being at church when her "children got saved." I watched with concern, half hiding because I didn't know if Mama liked what Dean and I had done.

Aunt Rose was Mama's oldest sister. Twenty-seven years and eleven kids separated them in the large family of fifteen. They were very close, so she could speak her mind to Mama without the volcano erupting. Amazing. Few on the face of this earth could talk to Mama like that and get by. Both of them spoke their minds easily.

Mama told her what we did was fine, but she made it crystal clear that she wouldn't be going or taking us to church. If we went to church, Grandma or Aunt Rose would have to take us. She said she'd never go again after some of those holier-than-thou church folks tried to cast the Devil out of her. That went over my head at the time, but the thought of going to church with Aunt Rose every time we came to her house for the weekend made me happy.

True to her word, over the years we only went to church when we visited Grandma or Aunt Rose in Georgia. Aunt Rose's two youngest boys, Chad and Brent, were accustomed to going to church every Sunday and naturally assumed when we were there that we would be going too. Mama never went with us but stayed at their house and waited for us to get back. She seemed to tolerate our religion as long as we didn't talk to her about it. We didn't.

Mama had her own kind of religion. She said "God" a lot, but it didn't seem very respectful. There were other words she phrased with it, which made Grandma upset. Grandma did respect God and worried about Mama's lack of it. Grandma tried on occasion to talk to her about it, but Mama usually got angry. She tolerated Grandma's admonishment but wanted her to hush about it. Many years later, I came to realize that Mama did not respect anyone or anything—least of all God. Maybe she felt He'd let her down somehow. She'd had a rough life.

She had her own philosophy about spiritual things too and didn't mind sharing it with her family and friends. She is very intelligent and a gifted reader and, like many, believed the Bible to be just a bunch of entertaining stories.

She loved to tell us her stories. She could craft and tell some amazing tales. Some of them were creepy and we believed them at the time. One of her creepiest was the story of her daddy's death. He and Grandma lived in southern Georgia, and we lived in South Carolina at the time.

According to Mama, on the night Grandpa died, Grandma appeared at our front door, calling Mama's name. Mama said it was black dark and storming. She hurried downstairs to open the door and let Grandma in—but she wasn't there. A day or so later, Mama got word that Grandpa had passed away. Mama often saw and heard things that weren't there and built stories around the incident to make sense of it. She believed Grandma was trying to tell her Grandpa had expired when she "saw and heard" her at our door. Mama told us she was glad he was dead and hoped he rotted somewhere. She had expressed her hatred for her daddy to us many times. I don't remember going to the funeral.

Mama expressed her views readily and easily. I agreed with some of them; some of them I didn't. I didn't agree with her about God or things pertaining to Him. That doesn't mean I was righteous, though. As I've mentioned, after I made my confession of faith in that little Baptist church, I only attended church once in a while, and I listened to unusual spiritual narratives at home. It is safe to say I was not too serious about my relationship with God. I'm not casting blame or rendering excuses; I'm just stating fact.

Eventually, I settled down and rededicated my life to God at another small country church with the young man who had become my husband. He knew the Bible very well and helped me develop a love for God and His Word. I found out that relationship was more important than religion.

Though my relationship with God strengthened after I married, I had always had a healthy respect for anything pertaining to God and Jesus. He seemed to have always been there, during the blessed times and the wild times. I guess I have to thank Grandma and Aunt Rose for that. I know He had answered their prayers, and, since my renewed relationship with God some years ago, He had answered a number of mine. Lately, my cries to Him detailed the increasing number and intensity of my nightmares, compounding fears, and deepening depression. Was the answer to my prayers Paul Thompson Counseling? It appeared so.

Paul Thompson Counseling was located in a renovated old house in Tallahassee, Florida, which was part of a nice, somewhat quiet area of town, down from the Old Capitol building. When we arrived, Anna went in for her appointment. The cozy remodeled living room provided a comfortable seat and plenty to read as I waited for my turn. The interior decorations spoke peace and serenity, a welcome change from the busy traffic a couple of blocks over on the six-lane avenue we scuffled through to get to Paul's office.

The restroom, located in the hallway between the waiting room and the counselors' offices, still contained charming remnants of its former

1970s décor. The small kitchen, white-glove clean, was always vacant until time for snacks or between-client cups of coffee.

After an hour, I heard the office door open and Anna's "See you next time." I grabbed my leather bag, stuffed in my still-ungraded papers (wondering why I'd brought them), and shouldered my purse. Load-balanced like a pack mule, I headed down the hallway. Nervous? Yes. Anna understood and gave me an encouraging look as we passed each other.

I unloaded and sat down gently on the edge of the burgundy leather sofa in Paul's office. He faced me, sitting in a padded swivel chair in front of a personal-sized, semicircular mahogany table that held a file folder, a pen, and a pad of paper. The softly lit room was quiet and pleasantly cool.

After he welcomed me and made sure I was comfortable, Paul explained the procedure for a new client. A normal session began with prayer, inviting Jesus to take part in the session. Difficult memories then open up in layers, like peeling an onion. The deepest hurts might take some time. We would deal with each layer until all was calm and peaceful.

Paul then asked me to give him a number from one to ten, rating the emotions he would call out. When he said, "Depression," I responded, "Six." *Who am I kidding?*

"Bitterness," Paul said.

"Ten," I answered—though I wanted to scream out, *"Fifteen ... twenty!"* I sincerely thought the bitterness toward the church was my biggest issue, probably because it was the latest of my hurts, the first layer. The focal point for the bitterness was the group of older men and women in the church who'd kept my family in bondage for years. "To be a Christian woman, holy, without spot or blemish before God," we were instructed, "you cannot wear pants, jewelry, or makeup. You cannot cut your hair. Hemlines must be respectably below the knee, and to make sure your armpits don't show, sleeves are a must in all shirts, blouses, and dresses. You are sinning if you cause a man to lust for you."

It's hot in Florida from early spring through late fall, so wearing dresses all of the time didn't seem like a big deal then. We wouldn't have to wear long sleeves, just a short sleeve would do.

There weren't regulations for the men's appearance. I guess they knew how to dress appropriately without a set of rules. We were taught to respect (obey) the men of the church, and they decided everything. My daddy had suffered so much from his domineering wife, so the idea of a man in charge was refreshing.

Some ideas seemed excessively harsh, I thought, but what was the harm? My Sunday school teacher, an elder in the church, told us we shouldn't wear anything in our house that we wouldn't wear to go shopping. I wondered what his wife slept in. I laughed when I thought of the "check and dash" procedure we used to get from the bathroom to the bedroom if we'd forgotten our clean change of clothes. I doubted anyone in his family would even attempt it.

"Public bathing" was another issue. The temperature in Florida can reach ninety-eight degrees before noon on most summer days. Swimming in the springs is how a Floridian copes with the heat. The church elders said, "If a group of women wants to get up at the crack of dawn and go to the springs to swim, that is fine, as long as they pack up and leave at the first sign of a man," which was usually about nine o'clock, the time the heat began to kick in. The water in the springs is freezing cold. Swimming in that cold water at the crack of dawn didn't appeal to me, so if I joined the church, from then on my summer cooldowns would consist of a kiddy pool and a water hose in the privacy of our backyard. Seemed like a small price to pay.

The church was a major component of my husband's life growing up. Grant's parents were faithful members, and when I married him, I knew it would play a large part in our lives as well. I wanted to teach the small children's Sunday school class, and joining the church was a requirement, so I joined and followed the church by-laws to the letter. I didn't do anything half way or gradually either.

No makeup? I am a strawberry blonde with blue eyes and blonde lashes and eyebrows. I felt I looked sickly and washed out without makeup.

"So what?" the elder church ladies said. They taught me that a godly appearance should be desired. Women "of the world" wear makeup so men will lust for them.

No jewelry? No problem. I owned only a few inexpensive pieces and rarely wore them. I didn't intend to buy more. We had begun a family; other needs came first.

At the time, wearing dresses in all circumstances only affected me. Our oldest was just a toddler. As she got older and then our son and another daughter came along, I continued to conform to keep peace in my family and the church. Peace. That was the goal.

When everything added up, the "small price to pay" turned out to be my freedom to be myself. As a result, I became a washed-out, beaten-down slave of the church. I was sure no man would lust for me! Eventually, not even my husband desired me. He stayed away much of the time—on purpose. Where was Jesus in all of this? He was speaking, but I couldn't hear Him for the booming voice of the church.

For years, my girls and I froze in the winter or looked ridiculous in dresses with leg warmers over pantyhose. We also faced the ridicule of playing sports in dresses or those hideous culottes, a cross between a skirt and shorts. Finally, I had had enough. I just could not see where

God fit into all of that, so I decided to be honest with Him. I could not continue to live a life I didn't believe.

All of the ridicule my girls faced at school burned in me. Their teachers called me on one particularly cold day to ask if they could buy pants for them; they thought we just couldn't afford them.

I had to tell them, "No, we don't wear pants." They were nice, but I could tell they thought we were idiots. I was beginning to think so myself.

Embarrassed and—in my estimation—powerless to do anything about it, I helped the girls be brave. I told them they were doing it for God. Really? Would God put little girls through that? If I couldn't understand it, how were these children expected to understand? My heart broke.

Time to get real, Carly. I knew it had to start with me. Though our son was unaffected, our girls were young and would, for a time at least, continue to follow my lead. My husband was right there, stuck with me in the mire of our obedience to the church.

The difficulty for Grant was not only in watching our girls suffer but also in battling his upbringing. His parents had no daughters, so the church regulations affected only his mother, who followed them to the letter. Grant didn't see why God had trouble with women wearing pants or makeup, but if the church said it shouldn't be done, then we were not to do it. He wanted us to live according to the regulations at first, but when the girls started school, he saw how they suffered and had a change of heart. Since he doesn't adapt to change easily, this was a real battle for him. Was his upbringing right or wrong? He certainly didn't want us to do something that would eventually send us to a place of eternal torment, as the church believed.

I craved peace, so I spent a lot of time in my walk-in closet. The quiet darkness enabled me to focus. When I first used the closet as a private place to pray, I didn't shut the door completely. Fear gripped me in the dark, but the sliver of light under the door made it less menacing. As I prayed regularly and felt the closeness of God, this closet became my favorite place to pray, though I still always checked for the sliver of light.

I went into the closet, pulled the door shut, and sat down by the shoes. After thanking God for all of the times He had helped me before, I then laid the whole situation before Him. I told Him I sat before Him naked, with no hair or gender. I was just "me." Forget the church; forget everything I had learned about what being a Christian is. I asked Him to show me what He wanted me to look like. Who did He want me to be? Was He happy with the real me? I needed to know, because I sure wasn't happy living the fake life. A scene opened in my mind like a movie clip.

Well-groomed and nicely dressed in a pants outfit, I stood smiling, talking to someone, possibly a coworker, about the goodness of God. We shared a small, modern office with computers, counter space, and shelves. I showed her something from a purse-sized Bible.

I hadn't even thought of pursuing a college degree, but I knew it was the life both God and I wanted for me. Excited, I couldn't wait to present the idea to Grant. He wrapped his arms around me and encouraged me to pursue my dream.

Right away God began to work on my behalf. Following His lead, I checked into local colleges and study programs. I had finished high school a number of years earlier and wasn't very confident in my ability to succeed in higher education. When I took the college entrance exam as my "make or break" step, I did well. I tested out of three beginning courses, giving me nine credit hours before taking a single class. This gave me some much-needed confidence, and with my family's encouragement, I began to pursue a college degree. Within five years of that prayer in the closet, I graduated summa cum laude from the University of Florida and began teaching in the public school system.

That day in the closet also began my rebellion against the bondage of the church. After prayer of his own, my husband agreed. We decided our family would dress comfortably, modestly, and in style.

Our girls, then eleven and five, were allowed to wear pants, have pierced ears, and cut their hair. They already owned pants. Friends and family bought pants for them, and I kept them; I guess I'd hoped they would wear them. My sister-in-law, Sheryl, a beautiful, stylish woman, gave Macie several bags full of matching outfits. Though Macie was twelve years her junior, Sheryl's petite frame closely matched Macie's at the time. We were thrilled with the new wardrobe.

After the girls' ears were pierced, Grant took them to get several pairs of earrings. He wanted to join in the fun. I took Macie and Anna to the beauty shop, where I had had my hair done as a teen.

The last time Macie's hair was cut was when her cousin cut off her ponytail on the school bus during their kindergarten year. As she got older, her hair became thick, naturally curly, and a beautiful dark brown. The hairdresser only trimmed Macie's hair because she liked it long. It hung in ringlets. When someone asked her who permed her hair, she'd say respectfully, "God."

A short pixie cut worked perfectly for Anna's cute five-year-old personality and very straight blonde hair.

The girls danced around like Christmas had come in October. My heart was overjoyed to see them excited to go to school. No more struggling to get them up in the morning.

My ears were pierced in my teens. I bought some jeans and dress pants, had my waist-length hair cut to my shoulders, put on some makeup, and acquired some inexpensive jewelry. I felt like a butterfly coming out of a cocoon.

Before the church elders asked me to, I resigned as teacher of the Sunday school class. A few of the old folks in the church thought we had lost our way and prayed for us. Others knew the regulations were too strict and change was needed in the church. They spoke in hushed tones about it, huddled in their small groups. Finally, the uneasiness spread, even to the upper level of the church-leadership hierarchy nationwide, and they realized the denomination would die if changes were not put into place. Glad to see the reformation of the church's policies but still bitter toward all those men and women whose strict rules brought so much unnecessary suffering and emotional pain, we canceled our membership with that church and attended elsewhere. I still felt a nagging, though, when I wore a sleeveless shirt. Would it ever go away? If a man lusts over armpits, isn't he the one who needs counseling instead of me?

"What about anger?" Paul asked. He waited for me to rate that emotion.

"About a two," I said. What was the point in being angry? It gets you nowhere. I couldn't point the anger at any one person in the church. It was too exhausting to be angry with all of them. Besides, I wondered exactly who had made up those rules. Not the local church.

As far as anger over other issues, I was livid a long time ago about the abuse I'd suffered as a child but evidently got over it. It's like a monster in my closet. I shut the door on it. If I'm reminded of it, I ignore it. I'm fine.

My siblings feel the same way. Through the years, we just didn't talk about it. We have always known we were abused as children. As the products of an often-absent alcoholic father and a mentally ill mother, we never knew what the day would bring. Though Dean and I, the two oldest of the six children, were more severely abused, our two middle siblings suffered quite a bit too. Punishment was plentiful; food and drink were scarce. As kids, we learned to cope with it. What doesn't kill you makes you stronger, right?

I thought every family had at least one parent who disciplined like ours did. Mama's discipline was brutal. With an extension cord folded to make four strands, we suffered deep, bleeding, purple and red stripes on our naked behinds, our backs, and the backs of our thighs, well placed so they would be hidden when we went to school the next day.

We had suffered, but so what? We turned out just fine. Well, most of us did anyway. Dean resides at a mental health facility in another state.

3

As my first session continued, Paul shuffled some papers while I sat on the sofa, feeling very vulnerable. Did I want to tell this man my deepest thoughts? Mentally, I reserved the right to withhold any information I didn't feel comfortable sharing.

As Paul had said, Christian counseling includes prayer, so I closed my eyes as Paul prayed, inviting Jesus to join in and help me to get to the issues that needed to be opened and dealt with. I immediately felt the presence of a friend—a good, faithful friend. I kept my eyes closed and a memory opened up.

> Ten or eleven years old, I stood by Grandma in the tiny kitchen of the small, two-bedroom, wood-framed house in southern Georgia where we lived. We were busy cutting up vegetables to go in a soup for supper and quickly discovered my lack of skill with a knife. I am left-handed and seemed to be very good at cutting myself instead of the vegetables. At that revelation, Grandma decided I should clean, while she cooked.
>
> In this memory, Mama was twenty-eight and very sick. Grandma, older than seventy, had come over to take care of Mama and us. Southern Baptist and very old-fashioned, Grandma believed there was only one way to do things: her way. She also stood by the old way of her American Indian

heritage, which dictated that only women should do work in the house or the yard.

The memory continued as I saw Dean, who, though eleven months older than I was, didn't have to do anything. While I washed dishes, swept the floors, and did whatever else Grandma said to do, he played outside and did whatever he pleased. She didn't like to see me idle, so I stayed busy. When I asked her why I was the only kid working, she explained that I was fortunate enough to be the oldest girl, and it was my duty to serve the family. It also was my duty, she said, to serve anyone who needed it, doing whatever I could for that person. I had learned earlier in my life to do whatever I was told—no argument and with few questions. Grandma said that everything I did had to benefit someone else; doing anything for my benefit alone would be selfish. Mama taught us that Grandma's word was gospel and was to be strictly obeyed—except when Mama disagreed with it, of course. Mama was fine with Grandma's teaching on the honor of servanthood.

Mama enjoyed reading and spent a good portion of each day with a book in her hands. Books, coffee, and cigarettes were three essentials at our house and came before food or clothing. Reading was Mama's escape—and our escape from her attention—but I resented it. I felt like a slave.

When we were old enough to do most of the housework, Mama divided the chores among us. At least Mama disagreed with Grandma about the girls being the only ones who should work. Dean and I were given the same chore load. Lori, age six, and Wendy, five, were so young that they only folded washcloths and picked up their clothes and toys in the bedroom. They liked helping. Dean and I hated it. April was three; Jake, one. They were part of the workload.

The work started as soon as we got home from school, usually a sink full of dishes to wash and the everlasting mountain of clothes to fold and put away. (I guess I thought the clothes washed and dried themselves.)

Perish the thought of missing school. I went to school, sick or not. Schoolwork was nothing, though, compared to Mama-work.

In this particular memory, Mama had been very sick. Grandma made me stay home from school for three weeks to help her take care of Mama. Dean didn't miss a day.

As I saw this memory unfold, I told Paul everything. He asked, "What emotion are you feeling in this memory?"

"Worthlessness," I answered. "Like a slave. I am only alive to do someone else's bidding."

Paul said, "Jesus, what would you like for Carly to know about that?"

The voice, the same one from the light, spoke.

"You are valuable; you are no one's slave. As a child you obeyed, but now you can choose whether you want to do something someone asks; you don't have to. Do because you want to, not because you have to. And always make sure the benefit to the person is greater than the sacrifice you make to do it. If not, say no."

Say no? To whom could I say no? My husband? He didn't ask much of me. My boss? Yeah, whatever. My children? After what they'd been through with the church, I couldn't say no to my children.

Only I could sense what Jesus was saying to me. These were inaudible words from deep in my spirit, coming to my mind. And I answered Jesus in my mind. Of course, Paul didn't hear my inner conversation, so I had to tell him. He wrote down everything.

Paul referred to what I'd said earlier when he asked, "Do you still feel worthless?"

"It's confusing; I'm not sure what I feel." Then I thought of Grandma telling me of my duty to serve everybody and anger flared. I told Paul about that.

"Can I ask Jesus to take the anger away," he asked, "so we can see what is under it?"

"Yes."

"Okay, Jesus, would you do that? Carly, tell me when it's gone and what you feel in its place."

The anger left immediately, and I felt the overwhelming emotion that Grandma and Mama owed me forty-something years of self-respect.

When I told Paul, he said, "That's called unforgiveness."

I learned that when someone owes me a debt he cannot pay, I carry it until I forgive him and give up the debt. If I forgive him but hold on to the debt, I have to keep forgiving him every time he comes to mind. To completely rid myself of the burden, I have to forgive the offender and give his debt to Jesus, who accepts the debt, pays it with His sacrifice at the cross, and sets me free from it. I receive from Jesus what was owed by the offender.

If that person has asked Jesus for forgiveness, he is already free from it. My carrying it only hurts me. If he hasn't asked Jesus for forgiveness, that is between the two of them. My forgiving the offender gets me out of the picture. It doesn't let the offender off the hook with God; it removes me as judge and gives God His rightful place as judge in the situation. I gave Jesus the debt Grandma and Mama owed me.

Jesus said, *"You are no one's slave. You can choose. You are not being selfish; do what is best for all concerned. Your needs and wants are important too."*

When I gave Jesus the debt, Jesus gave me self-respect.

My attention then focused on the bitterness against the church people. Paul asked me to keep my eyes closed and feel that bitterness.

As I did, I pictured the group I resented. I told Paul all that I felt in that moment. I saw the bitterness as a result of the pain they had caused my family. I felt I had a right to be bitter. I also sensed a residue of the bondage. That residue created a pang of guilt whenever I saw someone who believed in the old way. Most of the members of this group are dead, but there are still some people in churches of this denomination located in our area who swear by the "old paths." I feel they think I don't measure up.

Paul asked, "How does that make you feel about yourself?"

"It makes me feel second-rate."

"Jesus, how would You respond to that?"

He replied, *"You are not second-rate. You can make choices for yourself concerning how you look, dress, or act. There is a direct correlation between what you look like on the outside and who you are on the inside. Quit worrying about what people think, and just be yourself."*

Again, I faced the issue of having the right to choose. This time, though, it was about who I am, not what I do. For as far back as I could remember, someone else's opinion had governed my choices. Even though I rebelled against the bondage of the church long ago, I still felt a pang of guilt when I wore sleeveless clothes or cut my hair. That same guilt hung over me when I made any decision on my own, as if I shouldn't put what I wanted ahead of what someone—anyone—else might want.

Paul prayed for me. I told him something pressured me about the way I looked and dressed and other stupid stuff.

"What do you mean by 'stupid stuff'?" Paul asked.

I shared my obsessive/compulsive behavior about the silliest things. "I have a favorite spoon," I told him. "When I set the table for a meal, I feel guilty if I don't give that spoon to someone else. If I eat with that spoon, I feel selfish and miserable during the entire meal. And another thing—I never place anything on a Bible because that would disrespect it."

I have many Bibles and books. What a pain to make sure a Bible always lays on top in a stack of books. How would I know which Bible goes on top if I was carrying a stack of them? Did it matter? How stupid was that? And I felt guilt when I missed a church service, even though I had the flu. I suffered guilt, but my pastor expressed relief that I'd chosen to stay home, rather than sharing the flu with him and his flock.

"I feel pressured about sleeveless shirts, and above-the-knee shorts, and stupid stuff, which doesn't matter to anyone else but makes my life difficult," I said.

Paul asked me if that pressure had a name. I thought about it and "religious spirit" came to mind; I had heard some ministers talk about this. It is the attitude of getting caught up in rituals and legalism.

"Do you want to get rid of the religious spirit?" Paul asked.

"Yes! Of course."

So we prayed, and I gave it to Jesus. Then Jesus reminded me I still had unforgiveness toward those long-dead folks from the church. They owed me the freedom to make choices for myself. I forgave them and gave Him the debt. I no longer felt bitter, and Jesus gave me complete and total freedom to be myself.

I closed my eyes again and saw what appeared to be bowling balls with the little chains attached. I realized they were the old "ball and chain" worn by prisoners and slaves. As before, two of the balls rolled faster and turned into black balloons with black ribbons; then they floated upward and burst. I had a pretty good idea these were the slave mentality and religious spirit issues just dealt with. I felt lighter, less burdened, as if I had just been released from prison.

I told Paul about the scene I'd pictured that morning when I woke up.

"Do you still feel like a slave, alive only to do someone else's bidding?" he asked.

"No, it's rather strange, but I feel a bit empowered."

I had an appointment to get my hair trimmed in a few days, so while driving home, I decided I would get the haircut I wanted for the first time in my life, instead of trying to please everyone else. When doubt said, *"Yeah, right,"* determination said, *"We will see."* I resolved that if guilt did try me, I would never give in to it again.

On Monday afternoon after work, I arrived at the hairdresser's, ready to be transformed into the new me. As I stepped inside, I noticed a poster on the wall of a cute short haircut I had often admired but never thought would be for me. This time when I looked at the poster, I thought, *Why not?* Pointing to it, I told her I wanted that cut, except a bit longer. I'm not one for jumping off a cliff.

Evidently she didn't hear the "a bit longer" part. When she finished the cut and turned my chair so I could look in the mirror, my eyes widened and my chin dropped. After the initial shock, however, I loved it. A part of me nagged, *What will Grant say?* He liked my hair shoulder-length, and this would be a bit of a shock to him too.

My hairdresser's shop sits right across the street from the parsonage of the church I had attended for many years. After my haircut, I stepped out of the shop to go to my car, and a thought crossed my mind. *What if the pastor or elders see me? Will they approve?* This time, however, the answer came without pause: *Those who are there now don't think like that anymore, and it doesn't matter what they think anyway.* I felt free; I could almost hear the shackles pop open and fall to the ground. I got in my car. *What a great feeling! I really don't care what anybody else thinks.* At least, that was how I felt right then.

When my husband got home from work that evening, I stood at the kitchen sink, washing potatoes to cook for supper. He followed his usual ritual of taking off his steel-toed boots, unloading his dirty outer clothing by the washer, and coming into the kitchen to give me a kiss and ask about my day. He put his lunchbox on the kitchen island and turned me to him with a strange look on his face.

I looked at him, desperately wanting him to like what he saw. His opinion did matter to me. A lot. A quiet man, I knew he'd neither gush nor rant and rave. His words would be to the point. He looked at my hair and said, "I like it." I melted right into his arms. He hugged me as the tears welled in my eyes. He said, "It's different, but I like it."

"Do you really? You aren't just saying that because you know it's important to me, are you?"

"No," he replied with that little smile I love so much.

After my Thursday appointment with Paul Thompson, I shared the entire session with Grant as we relaxed that night, so he knew after my haircut on Monday that I'd battled for my right to choose. When I realized my husband was the only one who could set me back in this effort, I knew the "obey the man" thing lingered still.

I actually depended on his opinion. Not used to making decisions for myself about my appearance, I didn't feel confident that my choices were the right ones. My choices had been dictated by others for so long I didn't even know who I was. Grant had long tired of my constantly asking his opinion. His answer lately consisted of, "If you like it, I like it," or "Whatever you think." I hated that. I just wanted a clear answer so I could please him.

On Monday evening, as we sat in our recliners watching television, I caught him looking at me several times. I saw that little smile. I didn't know if he was proud of my making a choice or if he liked what he saw; either way, that smile eased my mind. I had dealt with the church bitterness and the slave issue, but I knew the transition to freedom would not happen overnight. I had to deliberately make choices every day.

After only one session, I thought the bitterness involving the church and the slave-mentality issue Grandma and Mama had given me summed up my problem. I didn't realize I'd only uncovered the first layer.

For the next few days, I made other decisions for myself and realized how liberating the counseling had been. I felt stronger. I actually felt like an adult!

In the days that followed, though I was still happy with my progress, the anxiety showed its ugly face again. The nightmares were horrible, and in the daytime, the panic attacks flared up. I had no idea what triggered them. Out of the blue, my chest tightened, and my fingers and toes tingled. My mind raced. I had no idea what terrified me. The unknown frightened me, so I panicked over panicking!

When I talked to my sister Lori, she said I needed to go back to Paul. She had uncovered many fears and issues in her life when she consulted him and was sure my anxiety was linked to our childhood, though she didn't go into details. I considered the child abuse just a fact of my life and didn't think it needed attention, but because the nightmares, the panic, and other disturbing thoughts continued, I decided to make another appointment with Paul Thompson Counseling.

Rather than just coping with these problems as I had done for a long time, I yearned to get the help I needed and be free. Lori was certainly happy and free from the depression with which she had struggled for years.

If the first session is any indication, I thought, *this is going to be easy.* I chided myself for ignoring my sister's advice earlier and visiting Paul. A few more sessions under his counsel, and I could live happily ever after.

I did not realize, however, hidden deep in the recesses of my mind were locked-away memories far more sinister than religious bondage and that this kind of therapy was far from easy.

When my father and my mother forsake me,
    then the Lord will take me up.
                                    —Psalms 27:10

4

"Another week is a long time," I told Paul, holding the phone with my shoulder as I wrote in my planner. My impatience showed while making the second appointment. I wanted to get on with it. Paul replied that two weeks or so gave me enough time to process everything accomplished in the first session. I didn't realize the healing happened gradually.

As I went through my daily routines, the change in my thinking surprised even me. I felt good about myself and found that though I still did most of what I'd done before, I felt different about why. I saw the concept of doing for others from a different perspective. I was not the world's problem solver. I didn't have to step in and do everything for everyone anymore. I would do only what I chose to do, after considering the consequences and weighing the benefit against the sacrifice. Choice: what a wonderful idea. I wished Grandma could have known this concept. Her life would have been so much easier. I felt good about my progress and looked forward to the second session.

The terrifying nightmares and the haunting daytime panic continued to grow in intensity. I am a sensitive person—things worried me that bothered no one else. At night, I often dreamed that someone wanted to kill me. The method changed and the scenery changed, but the dark horror of impending death remained. I dreamed of being choked, stabbed, or shot, and this took place in the woods, in a field, or a grocery store parking lot. I told Grant about the nightmares when they became more frequent. He thought perhaps I was too sensitive to the violence on television.

Grant's favorite television show involved crime scene investigation, usually including a dead body. He wasn't bothered in the least, but I could never watch the beginning of this show because every time a dead body appeared or I saw someone being killed, I had an anxiety attack. If I could catch it in time, I closed my eyes, blocking out the image. That helped, but sometimes no warning came, and the image I saw gripped me. After the crime was done and the investigation part of the show came on, I'd be fine—as long as they didn't show the dead body.

Some panic attacks were relatively mild, and I'd close my eyes, think of my job or some other distraction, and wait until my heart slowed back to normal, the tightness in my chest calmed, and my fingers and toes stopped tingling. Other times, though, it took my breath and crushed my chest so badly that I'd have to leave the room and get involved in some other task to refocus my mind. Thinking I was just an overly sensitive person, I'd manage the anxiety, stay away from crime shows for a while, and file it away as just a part of who I am.

Some days, car-wreck scenes flashed across my mind. In one scene, I even smelled the hot asphalt and saw the whitewall tires, as if a car had run over me. I asked God at one point if He was revealing my death. Does He even do that? More and more, that scene crossed my mind when I parked and got out of my car at the local country store. I told no one about this problem, not even my husband. As days went by, it became more and more difficult to shove these images to the back of my mind and carry on, business as usual.

As I sat in the waiting room before my second appointment with Paul, part of me counted the minutes until I could get to the source of my fears; the other part of me dreaded it. Paul usually took a short break between clients, so after Anna's hour, I chatted with her for a few minutes. She had made wonderful progress under his counsel, and I hoped I would do the same.

Paul, so personable and friendly, greeted me with a smile and "How're you?"

I gave him the standard "Fine," but thought if I was fine, I wouldn't be in his office. I dropped my purse on the floor, and sat perfectly still, waiting for him to finish looking at my file.

He held his pen over the notepad and asked me if I was ready to begin. I nodded.

As he prayed, thanking Jesus for His care and inviting Him into the session, my eyes welled with tears. I snatched a tissue from the box on the table. Realizing one would not be enough, I grabbed the whole box and placed it on the sofa beside me. Now I was ready. At least I thought so. Nothing could have prepared me for that day's session.

When Paul finished the initial prayer, he reminded me to tell him what I saw, heard, thought, or felt so he could write it down. As before, I immediately sensed my friend, Jesus. I felt safe in every way: physically, mentally, emotionally, and spiritually. Paul asked Jesus to guide the session, starting where He thought we needed to go.

From deep within me, Jesus said I had a bright future, and He wanted me to be free from the issues that tormented me. Then, when His blessings came, I would enjoy them to the fullest.

Wiping the tears from my face, I closed my eyes, and my mind surrendered to Him. As the memory opened up, I told Paul everything as it happened.

> I was about five years old, lying on the metal-framed, white vinyl-cushioned couch in the living room of our tiny two-bedroom

apartment in a low-rent housing development near the naval base in Charleston, South Carolina.

My dad was in the navy, on the job from five in the morning until after our bedtime at night, so we rarely saw him, unless we stayed awake in our beds and waited for him to come home. Each night after coming in from work and eating his supper, Daddy slipped into our room and gave each of us a light kiss on the cheek and the all-important "I love you" before he went to bed. I planned to stay awake on this night.

It was late in the afternoon. Mama had spent hours that day ironing Daddy's uniforms. I hated ironing days because Mama put the ironing board right in front of the television, and we had to watch it through the clothes hanging down. I learned long ago not to complain, though, because she got angry if I did. One thing I did not want was Mama angry. She had finished in time to put away the ironing board and watch her show, *As the World Turns*.

When her show was over, she had turned the television down and gone into the kitchen to start supper. Watching that world spin around at the end of the show always made me sick, so I closed my eyes. I knew she always had an eye on me, no matter what room she was in, and I wanted her to think I was asleep, so I remained still. She liked me when I was asleep. She'd told her friend that.

On either end of the couch were little tables that didn't match. Through drowsy eyes I focused on the lamp. Tall with a white base and an off-white shade, it sat on the end table closest to my feet. The afternoon light dimmed, and I thought about turning on the lamp.

With my eyes half closed, I noticed a movement. What appeared to be a white couch cushion came down on me. It

> covered my head and face and down to my knees. I was trapped between the two cushions. I tried to move but couldn't, as a heavy weight pushed down on the top cushion. I fought but was totally engulfed in and crushed by the white cushion. Worse still, I couldn't expand my chest to take in air. I wasn't afraid—I felt calm, as though this was routine. Soon, I gave up struggling, and everything went black. From a white cushion to a black nothingness ... white to black ... I felt I had done this before.

Only seconds passed, and there was a shift in consciousness. A different memory—we seemed to go deeper, further back in time. Jesus said I was about four and a half years old at this point.

I continued to tell Paul all I saw and heard in the memories. Desperately wanting to get on with it, I scooted up and sat on the edge of the sofa with my elbows on my knees and my hands over my closed eyes.

> From the bottom of the stairs, I looked up at the bathroom door. Only the light from the bathroom, which shone brightly around the slightly ajar door, breached the darkness. I was with someone, though I didn't know whom. As I began to move up the stairway, I heard someone say, "She's drowning us."

I gasped, and my eyes flew open. I saw the wall in Paul's office, but the terror still engulfed me. My arms flailed out as though I was trying to break free, and I spoke in gasps because of the ton of bricks crushing my chest, "Oh, no. Oh, no! She's drowning us." Those last words took my breath away, and I almost fell off Paul's sofa. I motioned to Paul that I couldn't go any further. I heard his voice try to calm my thoughts, but the terror continued to overwhelm me.

From deep within, I heard a soft voice call my name. *"Carly. Relax. You're okay. Just relax. It's all right."* Jesus's calm, firm voice came through and stopped the whirling of my thoughts.

I began to sob as I struggled to calm down and breathe normally. Paul said we should stop at this place in the memory. I readjusted my seating and gripped the arm of the sofa.

We talked for a few moments about what it all meant, and I continued to tremble. Something horrible had happened, and I knew about it. I tried to breathe slowly and evenly while I analyzed the facts aloud. "I am alive, so obviously she didn't drown me—or Dean either. He's still alive too. Lori, if she was born, would still be an infant. She is still living and breathing. Did we have another brother or sister I can't remember whom she drowned?"

Paul suggested we work on that same memory in the next session. "Don't think about it or try to get it to surface until the next session," he said. "There is a reason your mind wanted to stop at this place in the memory. Don't push yourself. Let it emerge on its own."

He prayed, although I don't remember the words he prayed. I still was too shaken up by the other stuff going on in my head. Anna drove home, and few words were spoken. I was so thankful for her quiet, reserved personality.

Later that night, in tears, I told Grant about the session. He listened intently and offered only an occasional "uh-huh" or "hmm." Just what I needed—a listening ear and a dedicated, trustworthy, and loving heart.

After I finished hashing out the entire session and threw away the handfuls of used tissues covering my lap, we snuggled down in the covers to go to sleep.

When I closed my eyes, I was staring through five or six inches of water. It reminded me of my toddler days when Mama washed my hair in the bathtub. ...

I was calm, waiting to be brought back up out of the water. After a moment, I thought, *What is happening? Why am I still under the water?* Panic set in. Mama leaned over me in the bathtub. One hand held my wrists to my abdomen, as she always did when she washed my hair, but her other hand—normally placed at the back of my neck—was pushing my chest down. I could move my legs, but that was all. I was pinned to the bottom of the tub. My chest hurt. I wanted to scream but refused to open my mouth. I knew the unspeakable would happen if I did. Full-blown terror began.

I began shaking and made a struggling, whining noise. Grant shook me and got in my face. "What's wrong?"

I opened my eyes and started sobbing again. I couldn't talk for a while, so he held me close. My mind continued to try to make sense of it all. *She tried to drown me. Someone must have stopped her. Did Dean push her back and release me? Did Jesus? What happened next?*

Every time I closed my eyes, I saw the same scene. I couldn't get past the terror and wept for hours. I finally told Grant about it. He continued to hold me, assuring me I couldn't have drowned. "You are alive and all right now." I rested in that thought, nestled in his arms.

Lori crossed my mind. I remembered that several years ago she told me about a memory she'd had in one of her sessions with Paul. The memory was of a little girl, terrified, and she felt certain that little girl was me. I'd never wanted to talk about our childhood, so at that point I declined to talk about it with her. I desperately wanted to talk about it now. I wanted to know every detail she remembered. How did she know the little girl was terrified? Was the girl in her memory really me?

Although it was late, I called Lori, and we talked for about an hour. I told her about the memory that had opened in Paul's office and what had happened when I closed my eyes to sleep. Lori did remember that she'd had a particular memory emerge in Paul's office—she'd heard a little girl screaming, terrified. She described being in a warm, closed-in space, and hearing a strong heartbeat. That is all she remembered.

Lori became very angry with Mama as I shared my memory with her. The terror almost engulfed me; it was so real I didn't know if I would sleep at all that night. "Every time I close my eyes I see water and go through the same process: calm, confusion, and then terror. Lori, it's awful!"

"When all the troubling memories are opened and dealt with, you will be a happier, healthier person," she said. "I promise."

"Why can't I just forgive everybody in one motion and get on with my life?" I groaned.

"It doesn't work that way," she said. "Remember, it's like peeling an onion, one layer at a time." Lori assured me she would be praying for me every day until I healed. I thanked her, knowing I needed prayers.

With only two weeks left of the school year, the work pace slowed considerably. School was my escape—I easily focused on my students. When the terror crept into my thinking at school, I refocused on a task, firmly shoving the terrorized four-and-a-half-year-old inner me into the farthest part of my mind. I couldn't let her govern my thinking at work.

At home at night, however, it was a different story. For ten days after my session with Paul, I cried for hours every night. The terror persisted. I felt helpless. I felt four and a half.

Refocusing at work soon became more difficult. The terrorized little girl weighed on my mind as I continued to function in my adult world. As the school year drew to a close and we were down to the last two days, the students were wild with excitement. Teachers scrambled to get grades turned in and year-end documentation completed and filed. Though it's always a time of mixed emotions for me, this year my inner turmoil compounded the situation. I loved my students, and they had been successful, but I yearned for the close of that last day. I needed the time off to focus on me.

A three-day teacher training session was coming up, scheduled for the week after the students' last day of school. If I had been a participant, I could've just gone through the motions during the session, but this time I was one of three trainers. I was weary from lack of sleep, as well as fighting the mental battle, and I thought about taking sick days, letting someone else do my part of the training. This was a difficult decision because I never shirk my duty and usually enjoy training workshops.

While I pondered that, a fellow teacher and good friend, who also went to Paul, asked me if I remembered his phone number—she needed to reschedule her appointment. She asked if I would call for her. I nodded and stepped outside the building for some privacy. When I heard Paul's voice, tears welled in my eyes.

"How are you doing," he asked.

"Not good." I told him the situation, and he prayed for me right then on the phone. He told the little girl in me to be calm and quiet for now and let the adult me work; we would take care of the terror in a few days at my appointment.

Immediately, I calmed. The little girl relaxed and went to sleep. Not only could I stay focused and do my part in planning and executing the training for the next few days, but I also looked forward to it. I wished I had called Paul earlier.

When I gave the other teacher her new appointment date, she had no idea of the importance of those few minutes I'd spent on the phone with Paul.

For the next few days I functioned normally. At night, I didn't cry for hours as before; I slept. Though my emotions were no longer raw, anguish still lingered deep inside. I kept myself busy, refusing to allow my mind to go there. I knew I would have to deal with the terror and anxiety. It wasn't going away by itself. I thought my Thursday evening appointment time couldn't arrive fast enough.

5

Anna and I decided to do some shopping near Paul's office before our appointments. We shopped, ate, and walked around the mall and then shopped and ate some more. I guess I thought the time would pass more quickly, and since I love to shop, I also thought it would be a good distraction from my internal issues. But my heart just wasn't in it that day. Anna had a few things on her list, so she shopped with a focus, while I plodded along behind her.

Finally, I was in Paul's office, and our session began as usual: greetings, his prayer, and my tears. Jesus opened the session by reminding me that my future was bright, something I needed to hear. It had been a rough few weeks.

We started with the memory that had opened up at home after the last session. ...

> I went into the water easily, thinking Mama was washing my hair. Then I became confused. *Why was I still under the water? Why was she holding me down?* I kicked my feet, the only part of me I could move. I felt panic and then terror.

The next thing I saw brought more confusion—a flurry of individual pictures, like a jigsaw puzzle poured out of its box. There were so many pieces, and I wasn't sure how it all fit together.

I told Paul about each piece the best I could. It was difficult; they were flashing so fast, like a strobe light—the dark stairwell, a bright white ceiling, a dark room with no doors or windows, a pale purple child on the floor with her back against the wall, Dean asleep on the white vinyl couch, Mama sitting by the tub. There were other such scenes, more than I could process.

Everything suddenly stopped. Jesus told me to relax.

I took a deep breath and repositioned myself on the sofa.

The scenes flashed more slowly then.

First scene: calm, under the water, then confusion, followed by terror. Everything went gray and then black.

I had been through those parts so many times in the last two weeks that I was ready to move on.

> As I went through the water and up to the ceiling, a light—brighter than any I'd ever seen—pulled me to it. Then, I found myself in the dark living room downstairs, where I stared at my brother asleep on the couch. He looked so peaceful. From there I proceeded to the bottom of the stairway and looked up at the bathroom door. A thin rim of light shone around the edges of it. I moved up the steps and realized I wasn't alone. My large companion said nothing, but his presence comforted me, as if I'd always known and trusted him. He led me up the stairs, through the thin sliver of doorway light, and into the bright white ceiling, where I watched the scene below.
>
> The bathroom was square, about six to eight feet wide. A white porcelain tub sat against the wall facing the door, and the toilet and matching sink with chrome fittings were on the left. On the right, a small wooden bookcase held towels and grooming items.

On the gray tile floor between the sink and the door lay a small child, her back to the wall. Her naked skin was a pale lavender; she didn't move.

Mama, wearing a dark navy full skirt and an off-white shirt, slumped on the floor by the tub, her forearms on the rim. She was round, like an apple, and big; she had a hard time moving around. She seemed to be talking to herself. Her back was stiff, and her face was turned toward the water in the tub as she spoke angrily through clenched teeth. Then she flipped her head and turned toward the child lying on the floor. Mama's body slumped again as she pleaded, her face so sad. Dropping her head, she sobbed with shoulders shaking.

As I watched, her head popped back up. Her face was angry, and her back stiffened. She turned toward the tub, and began again to spew saliva-soaked words through gritted teeth. Back and forth, she argued. I couldn't hear what she said, but I felt the mood change in the room from anger to sadness and back to anger again, every time she flipped her head. Mama was two people, fighting.

The small child lying on the floor had not moved since the scene began, not a muscle, not a twitch. The wall above her displayed a large wet mark. Obviously, the child had hit there and slid down to the floor, where she rested in a puddle of water. She had little or no hair.

"Lori!" I gasped. "Oh, no! She drowned Lori!" Paul kept writing. Lori had wispy, light brown hair as a toddler. When her hair was wet, it seemed to disappear. My heart broke for her. I kept my eyes closed as the memory continued.

I moved down toward the little girl and noticed she did have hair, wet hair, behind her head in a ducktail shape. It was auburn, like mine. I looked closely at the little girl's face. It was me.

The half-opened eyes stared. Cold and blank. The deep purple-blue lips were parted. I moved closer to her mouth, and in the next moment, I stood in a dark room with no windows or doors. All was still and quiet. Then I heard Mama sobbing and her pleading yell. "Carly! Breathe!" I obeyed. My body trembled and swelled.

On Paul's sofa, I opened my eyes and took a very deep breath. The terror subsided, but grief took its place. I realized my mother did indeed drown me at about four years of age. As the tears welled in my eyes, I questioned, "What kind of mother would do that? What could a four year-old child possibly have done to warrant that kind of punishment? Why didn't I stay dead?"

Paul wrote rapidly as I talked. When I stopped talking, he cleared his throat and said, "Jesus, what do you want Carly to feel, think, see, or hear about this?"

Jesus answered that had it been my time to go, I would have gone on to heaven when I went to the bright light in the ceiling. God's purpose in my life had not been fulfilled, so I was directed back into my body. Jesus assured me I was valuable and that Mama was very sick. She didn't realize the value of her children.

Paul asked, "Do you want Jesus to take the debt your mama owes you?"

"I have to think about it. What does she owe me?" Then I knew; she owed me life. She had snuffed mine out. God's intervention gave it back to me. She could never pay that debt. I forgave her, and we prayed for Jesus to take the debt.

I saw a large, low-sided, cardboard box with rocks in it. I took one of three large rocks and gave it to Jesus, who placed it at the foot of the cross. I looked back in the box. There were two more large rocks, several medium and small ones, some gravel, and some dust. Focusing on the two large ones, I thought, *This is not good. What could be as bad as drowning?*

When we ended the session, I asked Paul if I could have imagined the scene in the bathroom.

"No, the details are too vivid and complete, and the emotion is real," he said. "Believe me, in my line of work, I know fake." With a sad look, he added, "It really happened." He reminded me to call him if I needed him.

I glanced in the mirror at my red, makeup-smudged eyes. *Straight home*, I decided. *I don't want anyone to see me like this.*

I was glad night had fallen and also was grateful that the school year had ended. I needed the ten weeks of a teacher's summer to get over this.

Anna was concerned and asked if I was okay as she started the car to head home. I assured her I would be fine, though I don't know how convincing I sounded—to her or to myself. She respected my privacy and said no more. I breathed easier. I knew she cared for my mama, and I decided I wouldn't spoil that for her. I planned to get over this, and no one, except Grant, need ever know. Silent tears rolled down my cheeks for the entire two-hour ride home.

Memories continued as I rode. Flashes of scenes ...

> I screamed in terror as Mama tried to hold me. The Good Mama tried to console me, but I feared the Evil Mama, who could show up in an instant. Didn't she lurk there inside of the Good Mama, waiting for the right moment to pounce again?

In my bottom bunk, I stuffed myself into the farthest corner, holding my blanket wadded in front of me. I did my best to disappear.

I hid from her many times after that incident, particularly at bath time. I fought her every time she tried to wash my hair. Finally, she tired of the fight and told me I'd have to wash my hair myself—and that was fine with me. I'd lock the door.

Later that night, in the privacy of our bedroom, I told Grant the details of my session in Paul's office. I tried to stop crying. Impossible. Forget the box of tissues; by then I cradled a roll of paper towels.

"Do you really think you were dead?" Grant asked.

"Absolutely. There is no doubt in my mind. I looked into my own lifeless face."

He held me so tightly that I could feel his lips move as he prayed for me. I prayed too. Truth fought disbelief. The vivid terror I felt convinced me I had seen the truth, but a part of me wanted it all to be gone, like waking from a nightmare and realizing it wasn't real. I tried to convince myself it wasn't real. I finally succeeded, and at three in the morning, I fell asleep.

My body trembled and swelled. I came to, choking, gasping. I was naked and wet. Mama had my arm, pulling me to her. *No, get away! Stop!* I wanted to scream, but my throat wouldn't work. I fought to get away from her, but I couldn't. I threw up a nasty-tasting liquid. Again and again, I threw up. My throat burned. I tried to pull my arm away from her, fighting her. Now screaming. All of my strength went into each scream. My throat was raw, but I couldn't stop screaming. She was stronger. Everything went black.

I sat up, wrapped my arms around my knees, and tried to stop shaking. Grant still slept soundly. Good. No need for his sleep to be interrupted. Another nightmare. This time, however, I understood it.

The alarm rang at 5:20 every weekday morning. I'd normally get up, pack Grant's lunch, kiss him good-bye, and start my day. This was a weekday but far from normal.

Grant patted me and said, "Don't get up. I'll get something in town for lunch." After he dressed, he grabbed his metal clipboard case that held everything needed by a pipefitter foreman and turned to me. "Are you going to be all right today?" he asked. "I can stay with you if you need me." He picked up the pile of used paper towels on the bed and tossed them in the trash. The concern in his face gave me a clear picture of how bad I looked.

My face, pale from lack of rest, swollen and red from crying, tried to smile and lighten up. I promised him I would be fine. He hugged me tight one more time, kissed my forehead, and then left. We both knew I would call his cell phone if necessary.

Left alone, the enormity of what had happened hit me. I had to talk to someone. Who could I talk to who would understand and just listen, without forming an opinion about Mama? Who could I talk to about something this horrible and strange? Who'd not think I'd lost my mind? As I walked around the bedroom, talking aloud to myself, I realized I already looked like the village idiot, so I decided to call Lori and no one else. She understood crazy. We had lived it.

Impatiently, I waited until seven o'clock. I knew she would be up then, wrapped in a terrycloth robe, nestled in the small sitting room off her bedroom. In my mind's eye I could see her with a cup of coffee in one hand, the pages of her devotional held open with the other—that is her routine each morning. We are creatures of habit, and I found comfort in that.

Lori's summer hours each week at the college had changed from five days to four, with longer hours. She had every Friday off, so we had plenty of time to talk. I told her about the session. She listened intently, gasping every now and then. When I finished spilling it all to her, she said softly, "I am so sorry." Then her anger flared. She aimed a choice comment at Mama, which helped me. My emotions were raw, and I needed a normal person to feel my anger and pain and to validate them.

As a teacher, I had gone through crisis training, preparing me to aid students who go through either a personal crisis or a collective one, such as a teacher dying. I knew the steps of grieving, and in my mind, on that day anger replaced disbelief. Questions arose again. I blurted out, "How could she do such a thing? What could a four-year-old child possibly have done to deserve that?"

Lori calmed and reminded me that Mama was a very sick woman, so the incident probably wasn't linked to anything I had done. We talked then about Lori's memory and the likelihood that Mama's pregnancy with her had neared full term when this incident occurred. I recalled Mama's size in the memory and the difficulty she'd had moving around. How did she get me out of the tub? She and I alone occupied the room. The wet mark on the wall indicated I had splattered there and slid down to the floor, where I lay on my right side in a heap. Had she flung me there? So many unanswered questions.

After my call to Lori, I lounged around all day, praying and thinking. Disbelief and anger switched places over and over, like leap frog, and I sensed the dark cloud of depression moving in. I didn't want to tell anyone about this; I just wanted it to go away. It didn't go away, and when Vickie called, the dam broke and flooded all over her too. She listened and did her best to encourage.

Vickie is a wonderful, caring confidante. Though she is married to my cousin, we are more friends than relatives. She is one of my best friends, who also happens to live a walking distance from our house.

She was there for me when our younger daughter first came back to live with us; Vickie knows all of my dirt. Anna, at that time suicidal, could not be left alone. I would have had to take a year's leave of absence from my job to stay home with her if it hadn't been for Vickie. Vickie takes care of her seven grandchildren while their parents work, so she said Anna could stay with her and help with the kids. Anna loves children; in fact, childcare is her passion. She has known and loved Vickie since birth, so it was a perfect fit. After several months with Vickie and a number of visits with Paul, Anna was finally able to stay home by herself.

After my phone conversation giving details of the drowning to Vickie, I felt terrible. *So much for my plan to keep it to myself.* I prayed, feeling guilty that I had made Mama look evil to my husband, my sister, and now my friend.

That comforting voice broke in. *"You have to talk about this; you can't hold it in. Don't feel guilty. The truth is the truth, and you have to deal with it in the best way for you. Choose carefully to whom you talk, but do talk about it."*

My cousin Brent came to mind. I decided I'd call him that evening when he finished his UPS route. He is like a brother to me, but would he think I was terrible for talking about this? I was willing to take the chance.

Lori, Vickie, and Brent would become my extended support group. They knew how to listen with their hearts, offer comfort and prayers, and keep a tight lip.

6

Brent usually got home around eight in the evening, and by eight thirty, I had enlisted his ear and his heart. I told him I didn't want to hurt or belittle Mama; I just needed another point of view. I had already purposed in my heart to forgive, no matter the pain a memory caused. Brent agreed this was the best way to handle the situation. He also agreed I needed a support group and desired to be a part of it, assuring me that he and his wife, Glenda—his soul mate—would pray and keep our talks confidential. "You can call me anytime. I don't mind a bit. You know that," he said.

"Yes, I know. I just want to talk to someone who remembers, who knows our family, and who understands where I'm coming from."

We talked for hours that night, discussing the memories and our mamas' upbringing. I asked if he knew anything about the abuse. Brent, saddened but not surprised about the drowning, remembered that my siblings and I had suffered when we were little, but he didn't know it had gone that far. As we tried to figure out what could have driven her to be that way, he filled in some of the details he had heard of Mama's life as a child, things of which I'd only heard bits and pieces when growing up.

Mama's daddy, a huge man—head and shoulders taller than most—married Grandma when she was fifteen and he was thirty-four. He fathered seven boys and seven girls and carried his authority with a vengeance. Their first child, a boy, died when he was under a year old.

The other thirteen children were healthy and strong. The boys worked in the tobacco fields in that southern Georgia town, while the girls worked in the house and adjoining fields, taking care of the huge family's needs. Brent said his mama, the oldest girl and strong as an ox, didn't hesitate to get behind a plow. Everybody worked and carried a load, except my mama, who was too young.

Grandpa seldom had anything to do with Mama, but he ruled the others with an iron fist. They all feared him. He used whatever was at hand—a four-cornered tobacco stick, hoe handle, and later, a walking cane—to beat the boys and anyone else if his commands weren't followed. Mama bitterly hated him for beating her own mama.

Brent's mama, Aunt Rose, was the oldest living child of the family, and my mama was the baby. Grandma had given Grandpa those fourteen children from around 1900 through Mama's birth, about thirty years of childbearing. Grandma outlived her husband by fifteen years, and weeks before she died, I heard her broken voice declare he never loved her.

As I saw it, Grandpa never loved anyone. Grandma was his second wife. He had a daughter from his first marriage, but Brent and I never knew anything about her. Losing his first wife could have caused Grandpa to be angry and hard. Losing a first-born son at under a year old in the second marriage could've also hardened his heart. The life of a 1930s dirt farmer was difficult with little reward, and fifteen mouths to feed would have weighed heavily on him. During the Great Depression, life was difficult for everyone but far worse on families with no love.

Brent and I both remembered hearing stories of Mama having to fight off her brothers-in-law when she blossomed at an early age. Mama told me years ago that when she went to her daddy for help in fending off the advances of these men, he was too old to help her. He acted like he didn't know what she complained about and told her to "get out from under foot and go play." Grandma treated Mama as if it were her fault.

Three of her sisters, the wives of these men, weren't any help either. They slapped her and called her rude names when she tried to tell them the problem. Aunt Rose had married and moved too far away to help her. Her twin sisters weren't much older than Mama and didn't care. It was the1940s. Mama was a minor, scared, and alone. Developing a malicious side, Brent and I surmised, may have been her means of survival.

"Your mama had problems; we both agree on that," Brent said, "but she went too far in dealing with you."

I told him Paul determined that something bad had to have happened to Mama at an early age for her to have the mental issues she apparently had. "My emotions are so mixed up," I said. "Part of me hurts for Mama, and part of me hates her."

Brent understood. He wished he could have given me more information, but he was only six years older than I was and too young to realize at the time that anything that bad had happened.

His older brother, Chad, who often said he didn't know how Dean and I were sane, is ten years my senior and knew much more. Once at a family reunion, I asked Chad for details of the abuse, but he refused to tell me. Dropping his eyes and shaking his head, he said if I couldn't remember, I shouldn't worry about it. Leave it buried.

It became painfully obvious that some things wouldn't stay buried, no matter how deep they are or how hard I tried.

The thief comes but to steal, kill, and destroy.
—John 10:10a

7

Inside the stairway closet, the pitch-black darkness hung thick in front of my face. My hands slapped the closet door as I pressed my whole body against it. I couldn't get out. I begged Mama, "Please let me out. I won't do it again!" I had no clue what I'd done wrong, but it didn't matter. I just wanted out. My arm ached from being grabbed and slung into the closet. "Please, Mama, please. I don't like it in here. It's too dark, Mama, and hot. Please, Mama!" Something scraped the floor and clicked under the closet doorknob. Mama mumbled.

As my eyes began to adjust, I saw the slim crack of light at the bottom of the door. That shred of light revealed some of the contents of the closet. A heavy coat hung over my head. Beside it hung Daddy's uniform. Nothing new. The lamp from the living room was next to my feet. Grabbing it, I felt for a bulb. This time it had one. Holding the plug in my left hand, I ran my other hand along the wall, looking for an electrical outlet. Not one. I sobbed until I couldn't sob anymore. The crying and the suffocating heat caused my head to throb, so I stretched out on the tile floor, put my nose to the crack, and sucked in the precious cooler air from the living room. Finally breathing better, I fell asleep.

I was awakened by a noise near my head on the other side of the door. I sat up. My stomach hurt, my mouth felt like cotton, and my clothes were wet. Nothing new. As usual, I had slept right through the need to go to the bathroom. Once we were sent to bed we weren't allowed to get up, so wetting the bed while we slept was normal for us.

I followed Mama through the living room in the dim moonlight and up the stairs to the bathroom. The drink of water helped soften the rock in my stomach. She stripped me down, pulled up my clean underwear as I stepped into them, and sent me to bed. Curling up with my blanket, I was grateful for the softness of the mattress. When Mama let me out of the closet, darkness had already fallen, and Dean and Lori were in bed. She had forgotten me.

Paul asked if I felt any unforgiveness.

"Of course I do, but I know what to do with it." I forgave her, gave the bowling ball-sized rock to Jesus, and watched Him lay it at the foot of the cross. I saw the little girl, the five-year-old inner me.

Paul told me to ask her if everything was calm and peaceful.

I asked her. She frowned. Her face looked angry, and sadness poured from her eyes. "No, she's still upset, angry, and sad."

Paul wrote while more memories opened and spilled from my mouth.

I was in the kitchen, and from my view the wide silver rim around the dining table divided the room in half. I could easily slip under the table, but standing there, I could also see the glass salt and pepper shakers with silver tops. The sugar dispenser, also glass with a silver top, was half full. Mama sat at the kitchen table, crying. My stomach knotted. Her crying made me nervous because sometimes when she got upset, her eyes changed and bad things happened.

Mama's eyes normally were hazel-blue, but when things got unbearable, her eyes lightened to a silver color. She became a different person then. Cruel and mean, she seemed to delight in causing someone pain, as if it fed something in her.

I searched her blue eyes for something to tell me why she was crying. As I studied them, I realized she stared not at me but through me, a painfully sad stare. Before I could speak, a voice from behind me said, "Leave her alone; you can't do anything." Two large hands turned my shoulders and led me into the living room, where I sat, picking at my fingernails, my stomach still in knots.

Then, a different memory, same scenario.

Mama sobbed at the kitchen table, her hands covering her face. I wanted to know why she was so upset, so I kept asking. "Mama, why are you crying?"

No answer.

"Mama, what's wrong?"

No answer.

"Mama?"

Her right hand slapped me so hard and fast that I bounced off the wall beside her and fell backward onto the floor. My face was on fire. I got up and ran to the living room to soothe it on the cool vinyl couch. I turned to watch her; she still sat there. If she moved, I was going to hide.

Repeat the same scenario.

> This time, she cried softly. I didn't ask why; I just sat in front of her, waiting, wondering, and chewing on my fingernails. Then I whispered, "I love you, Mama." She smiled and let me hug her.

I asked the little girl again if she was calm and peaceful; she smiled, and Jesus said this was a good stopping place for this session.

That night I did not sleep well. At three in the morning, wakened by my screams, my husband shook me. He held me close while I told him my dream. In the dark of night, I ran from someone or something trying to kill me. Tired of running, I stopped, turned around, and went after the threat. I stood at the door of a place I didn't recognize and yelled into the night, "Come and get me. I'm sick of running!" Then I took off into the darkness, screaming with everything in me.

Grant cradled me while I shook, buried his face in my shoulder, and prayed for me. After closing my eyes and drifting back to sleep, the terror found me again. Grant said I whined most of the night. He kept waking me, hoping it would end. It didn't. At eight in the morning, I called Paul and made an appointment for six that evening. Somehow, I had to get to the bottom of this, and I knew it had something to do with Mama and Daddy.

The seed for Dean's hatred of Daddy was planted early and had grown through years of reinforcing circumstances. Dean, the firstborn, was weak and whiny. Daddy called him a baby and tried to wrestle with him and teach him to be a big boy. Mama told Daddy to leave him alone and stop hurting his feelings.

I loved tussling with Daddy. I'd sneak up behind him when he was sitting at the kitchen table, poke him in the ribs with my stubby finger, and run. He'd chase me, laughing and saying, "You better stop poking me. I'm gonna get you!" I'd make it to the white vinyl cushions of the couch in the living room, just as he caught me and tickled my ribs. It's the best memory of my childhood, and I still don't understand why Dean didn't find that fun.

Early in our lives, when Daddy came home from work, he listened as Mama grumbled and complained. Life wasn't easy on a seaman's pay. She constantly complained about never going out or having any fun. They argued; then he went to the bar. Later, his coming in drunk fired up the feud between them again. Sometimes the fighting went from verbal to physical. Most of the time they fought behind closed doors, and both came out scratched up and angry. After Daddy went to bed to sleep off the liquor, Mama told us about the fight and how we would be so much better off if he would just go away and stay gone. If life was so great when he was gone, why did she cry all of the time?

Once, when I was about eleven or twelve, they fought in the living room. We ran in to see what the commotion was about and saw Daddy straddling Mama on the floor. He had bright red splotches on his face and neck and wet brown stains all over his white T-shirt. Her empty coffee cup, still steaming, sat on the end table by her chair. She screamed at him. He told us to go to our rooms, and she told us to stay and see what a bad person he was. He let her up and went to change his shirt and put cream on his burns. She had a sly smile on her face. I turned my head. I learned early in life never to take sides or let her see my feelings. Dean always took Mama's side.

After that, Daddy became more and more scarce. He left regularly on six-month cruises, which seemed to suit Mama just fine. We lived on the naval base in enlisted men's housing. Mama received an allotment check each month and bought groceries at the base commissary. We had some food, and she was finally able to have fun.

She and her friends dressed up and went out to the base clubs on weekend evenings, coming in at one or two in the morning. She had two close friends who lived near us and whose husbands were also aboard a ship on the Mediterranean Sea.

Mama and these two women wore the same size in evening gowns. They had several. Mama said the chartreuse green one was hers. It was the prettiest dress I had ever seen. Someone must have given it to her as a gift. She couldn't have paid for it because there wasn't even enough money for our school clothes or shoes.

Everyone looked forward to the weekend. Mama and her friends gathered at one of their houses, did each other's hair and makeup, and helped each other dress. I have to admit they were beautiful when they went out. I was sure no one at the club looked as good as they did. Mama said I was old enough to babysit her friends' kids. I could call base security if needed. Dean stayed home with our siblings.

During the day Mama took Valium for her nerves and drank coffee with these friends. She laughed a lot when she was with them, and we did our best to stay out of sight. Not all days were happy, though; at times, she complained of migraines and slept for days in a dark bedroom. I worried that the pills had become more of a problem than a cure.

During one of these episodes, I went into her bedroom in the middle of the day to ask her about something and found her in the dark, blinds down, curtains drawn, a wet washcloth draped over her eyes and forehead.

I spoke softly, "Why do you have it so dark in here, Mama?"

She said, "I have a migraine. The light hurts my eyes. What do you want?"

When my eyes adjusted, I saw the pill bottle on the bedside table. "Did you take your pills?"

"Yes. What do you want?"

My heart broke. I didn't even understand it myself, but I told her, "I want you to get better. I want you to stop sleeping all the time and come out of the dark. We need you."

She took the wet washcloth off her eyes, sat up, and smiled. She looked like death warmed over, but she said, "You're right. I do need to get better. I think these pills are causing the migraines." She handed them to me.

I walked out of her room and flushed the pills down the toilet. I was twelve.

When Daddy returned from a cruise in the Mediterranean, bringing Mama gifts from Italy and Greece, the atmosphere at home was great for a while.

One time he won the anchor pool. He explained, as he fanned out the forty twenty-dollar bills, that he had guessed the exact second the anchor would hit the water when the ship docked. That stack of green had Mama and Daddy both grinning.

They bought a lot of groceries and then went out to the clubs and had fun. We were happy to babysit. Life was good.

Then, after a week or two, it was back to the same old story. They fought; he left. Later, he came home drunk.

We thought things would get better when Daddy retired. Mama convinced us that the problems in their marriage all hinged on Daddy's drinking. When he drank, it made her crazy. (I suspected it was the other way around.) He promised us he would not drink another drop of alcohol when he retired, and he kept that promise, in spite of all he had to deal with.

8

"Ninety-nine bottles of beer on the wall, ninety-nine bottles of beer, take one down, pass it around, ninety-eight bottles of beer on the wa-a-al-l-l! Ninety-eight bottles of beer on the wall, ninety- eight bottles of beer …"

Rolling down the highway, we belted out the song we'd learned on the base from other navy kids. Mama hated it, but to us, it was just a song. Daddy smiled. He rarely said a word about anything we did. Mama ran the show, and we all knew it. We had already worn out "She'll Be Coming 'Round the Mountain" and "Row, Row, Row Your Boat." After singing those once, I had had enough, but the younger kids kept it going. Finally, they sang her around the mountain and had the boat row-row-rowed into a dream state, so we took on the wall of beer.

We tried to convince Mama the song had merit. At least with the bottles-of-beer song, we had to think. The song changed with each round, and the younger kids could practice their numbers from one hundred down to one. She wasn't convinced and made us change the name of the drink to Coke, which doesn't quite roll off the tongue like the word beer, but it was still fun to see if we could get all the way down to "one bottle" before we arrived at our destination. We never did. Either Mama came down with a migraine, or our throats wore out first.

It was summer in the early 1970s. We were on our way to Florida from Tennessee, where Daddy had spent his final four-year stint in the navy. Mama and Daddy decided that since we had to travel anyway, we might as well use the occasion as our first family vacation. The route they chose cut straight east across Tennessee to Gatlinburg, where we'd spend the night. The next day we'd head south on Interstate 75 through Georgia, back to northern Florida, where Dad had inherited property. We planned to spend many years enjoying the sun and fun.

I was fifteen and ready to stay in one place. I had gone to eight different schools in ten years of schooling. Sometimes we just moved across town to a less expensive rental house in a different school district; other times, Daddy's transfer took us to a new city or state. Either way, I left friends behind every time.

Six kids, two parents, and a pair of German shepherd puppies sailed along the Tennessee highway in a gold-colored, late-model Pontiac Catalina station wagon. The middle seat faced forward like the front seat, but the backseat faced the vehicle following us. The rear-door window spanned the width of the car, and with the glass rolled down a nice breeze flowed steadily through the car. To this family of eight with two dogs on a long road trip, ventilation was important.

In the backseat, we enjoyed watching the drivers of the cars following us. Cars didn't follow too long or too close, especially if one of us had a mischievous idea. I thought spitting wet paper balls through a straw was nasty, but I had siblings who thought it fun. The truckers, too high up to notice the wet paper, seemed to enjoy the antics of kids pulling their arms down twice to signal them to blow their trucks' horns. Three of us could lounge in that backseat comfortably, so Dean and I usually took turns and shared it with two younger and smaller siblings. For me, other than the obvious distance from Mama, the best thing about the seat was the view. We had a full 180-degree view of where we'd been.

The singing entertained us for a while, but everyone quieted when the view grew more interesting. Daddy's naval career had kept us close to the coastline, and flatland was all we knew until we moved to Tennessee. We had seen some foothills on the trip from northern Florida through Mississippi to Tennessee, but nothing compared to the majesty we witnessed on this trip. With wide eyes and mouths agape, we absorbed the scenery. The highway cut into the side of the mountain, revealing the layers of shale and other rock towering above us on one side and the mile-deep, forested canyon plunging below us on the other. We rode on the side of the highway closest to the canyon. Seeing only the tops of the trees took my breath away and made me nervous. I looked for highway railing—none. A driver's inattention for one second could prove fatal. Self-preservation caused me to cut my eyes to the front seat. To my relief, Daddy was driving.

When we arrived in Gatlinburg, Daddy checked us into a hotel perched over a narrow mountain stream. Lori and I decided to do some exploring when we took the dogs out for their walk. We had never been to such a place. Just outside the door, a walkway led around the side of the hotel, where a wooden bridge arched across the stream. The dogs, of course, headed straight for the water, so we waded in the shallow stream with them. Cold. Ice cold. Kind of took my breath away, but it was summer so we enjoyed it, laughing at each other and the faces we made when the cold water hit us.

Upstream, in a wooded area by the hotel, we discovered a waterfall cascading down over large, beautiful mountain rocks. Flowing downstream rapidly, the water smoothed the rocks, making them perfect for folks to sit on—for a moment. The icy water discouraged a long sit. In spite of the cold water, this place was a natural wonderland to me. The rustic beauty of the area lifted my spirits as the sound of the waterfall soothed away my stress, convincing me this move was truly the beginning of a new life for our family.

Mama seemed happy. Daddy was relaxed, looking forward to retirement. He talked about the home they had built on the ten acres

Daddy inherited from his dad. Though his dad, Perry, had died many years earlier, the property had been kept for Perry's children by an uncle until they grew up and could claim it. In the '60s, Daddy claimed his inheritance and, with Mama's input, had a three-bedroom, one-bath block-and-brick home built on the property. A steady stream of renters brought in a bit of added income until he retired.

Daddy couldn't wait to get to his little bit of heaven and plant a vegetable garden. As a career commissaryman in the navy, Daddy was educated in the field of nutrition and health. Good health could be maintained, he often declared, with a wide variety of fresh fruits and vegetables and some venison. All of this could be obtained on his ten acres. I was as excited as he was.

Our two hotel rooms became one as we opened the adjoining door. With both televisions on, though, the noise soon reached overload, and Mama closed the door. I didn't blame her. A noise level that high would have annoyed Mother Teresa. The setup was great because if someone didn't like the noise level in one room, he or she could go to the other. The room Mama with her migraine occupied was always quiet. Each room had two large beds. The two boys slept in the room with Mama and Daddy, and, as usual, we four girls had the other room all to ourselves. We didn't have to go to bed early either. We watched a movie and, one by one, fell asleep.

After a good night's rest and a leisurely breakfast, we piled back into the Pontiac and headed south to Florida. We arrived in pitch-black darkness. Inside the house, we rolled out the sleeping bags and spent the first night with no electricity, no water, and no screens on the windows. The woodland sounds of frogs, crickets, and mosquitoes buzzing in our ears welcomed us home.

Retirement meant many new experiences in rural northern Florida and though I looked forward to it, Dean didn't. He wasn't one to try new things. Daddy had been raised in the woods and loved every part of the experience, but Dean was a city boy. He let us know he hated the woods. Daddy thought Dean would learn to enjoy it and wanted to teach him what he knew about hunting, fishing, and such, so he often took Dean with him.

One time when Dean and Daddy went squirrel hunting, Dean shot one and ran over to pick it up. Daddy, several yards away, yelled, "Wait! Don't touch it 'til you make sure it's dead." Dean was so excited he picked it up anyway. The wounded squirrel bit him, and Daddy laughed at the way Dean was dancing around with the squirrel flopping from his finger. Daddy helped him get it off, and though Dean wasn't hurt, he was furious because Daddy had laughed.

Mama got angry too because Daddy laughed when he told us about it. The thought of Dean's dancing around, dangling an almost-dead squirrel from his finger, was indeed funny, but Mama's anger snatched the smile right off our faces.

Daddy enjoyed the retired life: hunting, fishing, growing his garden, and sitting on the porch with a cup of coffee in the evening. Mama had the car most of the time, so fishing was only on weekends, unless we wanted to walk the three miles to the river. Daddy did. None of us cared to. But hunting and other activities were readily available on the ten acres.

Dean hated our life. He especially shied away from anything to do with Daddy. Some of us, though, enjoyed being with Daddy. He was usually quiet but answered questions between sips of coffee if we asked him anything. We'd sit on the porch when night fell because our house didn't have air conditioning. It was cool and peaceful, watching the fireflies flicker.

We also enjoyed the fruits of Daddy's labor in the garden: huge red tomatoes and baskets full of delicious green beans, squash, cucumbers, and okra. He knew how to grow a bountiful garden and how to prepare those vegetables to keep a family healthy.

Daddy was indeed a great cook, but he struggled with cooking for eight instead of the twelve hundred sailors aboard a ship. Before he retired, I had watched him plan menus for ships going out for months at a time. His reports and menus enabled those who were responsible for the ship's stores to acquire the right amount of meat, fruits, vegetables, and staples needed for a lengthy cruise. We never went to bed hungry and ate a lot of leftovers.

At forty-two years old, he still had plenty of get-up-and-go too. Occasionally, he'd ask one of us to help him with something, but most of the time he did the outdoor chores by himself. We did the household chores, like washing clothes, vacuuming, dusting, and after-supper dishes. We four older kids took turns, dictated by the calendar posted on the refrigerator, so the workload was easy.

Mama got a night-shift job at the local wood mill, pushing boards through a planer, to supplement Daddy's retirement income. Millwork is tough, and she had every right to complain when she came in from work with huge blisters on her hands. Daddy listened and helped her but rarely said a word. They didn't fight anymore. Mama had made some friends on the job and seemed happy to be out of the house, away from Daddy and us. In the daytime, Mama slept, Daddy worked in his garden, and nine months of the year we went to school.

In the evening, while Mama worked, we played cards and board games or watched television after homework was done. Daddy drank his coffee on the porch, while his favorite music, *Ernest Tubbs's Greatest Hits*, played on the stereo.

9

One evening in Paul's office, I shared what I remembered about the night Daddy and Dean had their last argument. At seventeen, Dean thought he could do as he pleased. Daddy told Dean to help him with something in the garden, and Dean refused. Daddy didn't ask much of us, and the rest of us did whatever he asked. Dean hated Daddy, though. And for Dean, everything came to a head that night.

Daddy had been retired from the navy for just over a year. That hot summer morning, all of us except Daddy wanted to go swimming. He liked the peace and quiet of being home alone. He always said he had too much to do and couldn't go. "Y'all just go ahead," he told us.

Mama took all of us except Dean to the springs—he got a ride with his friends, and he went home before we did. Dean later told me that while he rummaged through the refrigerator, looking for a snack, Daddy asked him to help with the watering system in the garden. His insolent *no* brought a sharp look from Daddy, who told Dean he wouldn't put up with disrespect. He grabbed Dean's arm and pushed him out the door to the task. Dean fought back, hitting Daddy, and broke Daddy's nose.

When we got home from the springs, Daddy was angry, his nose swollen and purple, and Dean was gone. Daddy said he fled into the woods. He picked up the .22-caliber rifle and told us he was going to find Dean and teach him a lesson. Mama grabbed a carving knife from the kitchen, stuffed it in her purse, and took off right behind him.

Dean slipped back into the house before Mama and Daddy came back, and when he told me what had happened earlier, I wanted to say, "Why didn't you just go out there and help him?" But I kept my mouth shut.

The situation appeared to be stable, but as soon as Daddy walked in the door and saw Dean, he put the .22 back in the corner of the living room and charged at him. I'd never seen Daddy that angry. Dean fought back, and they tumbled to the floor. Though they were about the same size and weight, Daddy certainly had the upper hand. This time, all of us were afraid and tried to separate them. We pulled on Daddy and screamed repeatedly, "Daddy, stop! Please stop!" He had a solid grip on Dean. Mama told me to get something to hit Daddy on the back of the head. In the kitchen I grabbed the first thing I saw with a handle—a large knife. I didn't even realize what I had grabbed.

Mama said, "Not that! We don't want to kill him!"

I ran back and, with purpose this time, grabbed a long-handled pot from the dish drainer.

Mama said, "Don't just stand there! Hit him with it!"

I tried to summon the courage to hit Daddy. I could see how angry he was with Dean for hitting him earlier. I sure didn't want him to take the pot away from me and hit me with it. He had never hit any of us, but I'd never seen him that angry either. Terrified, I hit him on the back of the head. The blow wasn't hard enough to kill a mosquito. Of course, it didn't faze him.

Mama continued to beg Daddy to let Dean go. Finally, out of breath, she slumped. Clearly, she was at her wit's end. I watched her change. She stiffened and became a different person, no longer out of breath but strong and firm. Through clenched teeth, she said to Daddy, "I will kill you."

I thought she was just saying that, one of her off-hand phrases, but this was not off-hand, and looking into her eyes he believed her. Like a trapped animal, he backed toward the door and left. I heard the car speed away. Dean got up and went to the bathroom. We all took a deep breath.

When Daddy came back, he parked at the end of our ninety-foot-long driveway and sat there. The sun had just gone down, and the streetlights came on. I waited for Daddy to come in. Puzzled, I looked out the front window and saw the car but not him. Why would he leave the car at the end of the drive instead of pulling up and parking it by the house?

"Mama, where is Daddy?" I asked.

"He's walking around the house, looking in the windows." She was sitting at the dining table, calmly smoking a cigarette. "He's got a gun, and he plans to pick us off one by one. Just sit down and shut up."

I looked for the two guns he owned and saw them in their place in one corner of the living room. I thought maybe he had another one I didn't know about, so I slumped on the floor by the refrigerator, waiting for my turn. I watched the windows near me, hoping to at least get a few seconds warning so I could brace myself, resigned to accept my fate.

Soon, another car pulled up next to ours in the driveway. I saw the headlights shine through the front window and got up in time to see Daddy sit up, exit our car, and talk to the sheriff's deputy.

After a few minutes, they both came into the house and sat down with Mama to discuss the situation. Waiting just out of sight in the hallway, I overheard Mama say, in a very sweet tone, that it was just a misunderstanding. The officer talked to both of them, and they agreed to put it behind them. When the officer left, Daddy went to the garden by himself to set the watering system for the night. He wasn't gone long.

When Daddy came back in, he saw the guns were missing and asked where they were. Mama wouldn't tell him. For the next few hours he kept everybody awake as he tried to find the guns. He stomped down the hall, beating on the walls with open palms, yelling, "No one is gonna sleep in this house tonight 'til I find those guns!"

Mama had given me the shotgun while Daddy was out in the garden and told me to hide it in the bed with me. We four girls shared a room, and Daddy rarely crossed the threshold. He had never come near my bed. I was sixteen, and he respected my privacy. Somehow, that didn't matter in that moment. Mama had convinced me that if he found the shotgun, he would kill all of us. I believed her. Daddy had never acted this way; it was obvious to me that he had lost his mind.

Wild-eyed, Daddy barreled into our room, asking us if we knew where the guns were. No one said a word. His voice cracked as he told us he didn't want to hurt anybody; he just wanted to know where the guns were.

Pulling the three-inch blade from the pocketknife he used to clean his fingernails, he said, "If I wanted to hurt you, I could use this."

We stared. Nobody moved. He put the knife back in his pocket and pleaded. We continued to stare. I was sweating under the blanket with the shotgun under my left arm, streamlined down my body. With a look of defeat, he exhaled, dropped his hands, and walked out.

After gathering a clean set of clothes, he went into the bathroom, and the house got quiet. Too quiet. I left my bed and went into the living room, where Mama sat in the dark. The .22-caliber rifle rested across the arms of her chair. She had full view of the hallway.

I knelt down in front of her and asked, "What are you doing?"

She told me the same thing she had told us many times after fights they'd had. "We will be better off with him gone." She spoke plainly and didn't bat an eye.

I thought she was just going to run him off by pretending to shoot. She had found ways before to make him leave.

"Go to bed," she said.

I did.

After showering, Daddy stepped out into the hallway, heading toward their bedroom. From the living room, Mama fired.

Daddy wheeled around, begging, "No, honey, don't."

She fired again. He fell back into the bathroom.

April, only eight years old, jumped out of her bunk, shaking. "Is he dead?"

Mama said, "No, but he will be in a minute."

I jumped out of my top bunk and grabbed April. I didn't want her to go into the hallway. I sent her back to her bunk, and then I covered my ears. The gurgling sounds I heard as Daddy tried to talk were more than I could bear. Moments later, he was dead.

Mama stood in the hall, looking at Daddy. Dean stood there with her. She handed him Daddy's large hunting knife and said, "Here—cut my arm with this so it looks like he stabbed me."

Dean took the knife but almost dropped it. "I can't, Mama."

"Do it!" she said firmly. "If you don't, I could go to prison for a long time."

"I can't, Mama. I just can't," he whined.

Mama took the knife, stabbed her own arm twice, and put the knife in Daddy's lifeless hand.

Dean asked, "Can I go get someone now?"

"No! We'll wait a few more minutes to make sure he is good and dead." She went into the kitchen, and Dean went into his bedroom.

In disbelief, I took a step closer to the bedroom door. Seeing Daddy's feet in the hallway and the rest of his body in the bathroom, my chest caved in. Jake, seven years old, flew by me from the boys' bedroom into ours. I closed the door. I pulled all of the younger siblings onto the top bunk with me, and we held each other.

April kept saying, over and over, "Everything's gonna be all right."

I sat there, believing none of this was real.

Mama finally sent Dean to get the nearest relative, who came with a deputy. Through my bedroom window I overheard our uncle tell the deputy that Daddy had called the law from his house the previous evening. He added, "If I'd known this was going to happen, I would have kept him at my house."

It was three in the morning, and our yard was filled with people. My four younger siblings and I climbed out my bedroom window and into the yard—we'd been forbidden to go into the hallway, but some needed to use the bathroom. They stepped into the woods, and I kept an eye on Mama as I waited by the house for them. A different person now, Mama walked around, laughing and greeting everybody.

Moments later, Dean and I stood together near a tree. I said, "Mama's welcoming people and acting like she's at a family reunion." Clearly, she had lost her mind.

"I know," Dean said. "Play along."

I just shut my mouth. *We are the crazy family.*

Later, the sheriff's deputy hauled her off to jail in a squad car, and our aunt and uncle took us to stay with them up the road. It was about five in the morning. They sent us to different rooms in their huge house and told us to get some sleep. *Yeah, right.* It was summer, but I shook like I was freezing to death.

At six o'clock, my cousin showed me where their house phone was, and I called my then-boyfriend, Grant.

"Hey," he said. "What's the matter?" He knew I wouldn't call him that early unless there was a problem. I knew he had to be at work at seven.

"Mama killed Daddy." I didn't know how else to say it.

He grunted and whispered, "How?"

"Shot him." Plain and simple. "We are at our uncle's down the road."

He knew where. "I'll be right there."

He was twenty years old but still lived with his parents, and as I hung up the phone, I heard his mom question him. I guessed that he didn't tell her what I'd said but would tell her when he got back. About fifteen minutes later, he drove up. I was out the door before he could get his truck door open. He looked like he'd dressed in a hurry. No socks. His shirt wasn't buttoned completely.

He couldn't believe what happened and didn't know what to say, so I did most of the talking. A deputy showed up soon afterward and said we were not to talk to each other. Grant's eyes and slight shake of his head told me to be careful when I answered.

I said, "Okay, thank you for letting us know."

The deputy made Grant go home.

The next time I saw Mama, she was stepping out of the squad car in handcuffs at Daddy's funeral. She wore a navy blue shirt, a dark green skirt, and high heels. My siblings and I didn't get to say much to her. All of us sat on the front pew, a few feet from the open casket. Daddy wore an azure blue polo shirt, black pants, and peaceful look. He was the only one who did.

I had a friend whose father was the jailer, so after the funeral, I went to stay at the jail living quarters with my friend so I could be there for Mama. The rest of my siblings went to southern Georgia to stay with some of Mama's family.

By staying in our hometown, I could take care of Mama's needs and still see Grant. When Grant took me back to the house to get clothes for Mama and me, he gathered the bloody towels out of the bathroom so I wouldn't have to see it.

"My mama will wash them," he said.

I shook my head. "Just throw them away."

We picked the vegetables from Daddy's garden. Grant was amazed at Daddy's green thumb. He never judged any of my family and could not have been more supportive. We took the vegetables back to the jail kitchen, and they were used to feed the inmates. It was a six-week stay for both of us.

Mama pleaded self-defense, saying Daddy was a dangerous schizophrenic who had lost his mind. Even though I heard them say the knife was in the wrong hand for Daddy to have stabbed her, and Dean had to spend time in jail as an accomplice because of something he'd said, Mama was acquitted of the murder charge. The military records were used at the trial. Though I testified at the trial, they kept the records from my view. I was asked if I felt Daddy had lost his mind. Yes, I thought he had. But so had Mama. They didn't ask me about her.

Dean was forever changed. We all were.

I married Grant a few weeks after Mama was released.

Twenty years after Daddy's death, our pastor helped me grieve. I had stifled the grief and buried the pain. There were so many changes in my life to work through in the immediate aftermath of the murder that I did not allow myself to grieve. But after twenty years, nightmares about that night were robbing my strength, and good memories of him baffled me, so I talked with my pastor. He knew nothing about Daddy's death—he had only pastored there a few years—but knew God would be able to help me. I was so confused about my feelings. My younger siblings never knew the good Daddy I knew, and what I remembered became so distorted I didn't know what to believe about him. Mama had killed him in his children's eyes long before death claimed him that night.

For sanity's sake and at the urging of my pastor, I forgave Mama and moved on. Nothing could be done to bring Daddy back. I wish I could've done something to stop her. If I had tried, though, would she have killed me too? We'll never know. I told myself, *It happened. Nothing can change it now. Deal with it.*" I pretty much thought I *had* dealt with it.

Eighteen years after that pastor's counsel and my forgiving Mama, some of the more agonizing moments of that horrible night still hung on. That moment when I sat on the floor by the refrigerator, waiting to be shot in the head, flashed through my mind again in Paul's office.

He said, "Jesus, what do you want Carly to know about this?"

Jesus told me that only Mama had ever wanted to kill me and that no one wanted to hurt me now. Not even her. I reminded myself that Jesus doesn't lie.

10

Several years after I began my healing through counseling, I actively sought copies of Daddy's official military records so I could know the truth for myself. The records Daddy had been given when he retired were now scattered, but I could order a complete set. After a difficult and lengthy process, I finally obtained copies of all the documents in his file from the National Archives.

Excited, I read through the documents and began to remember the real Daddy. He had commendations from his superiors for things he did well. In one incident, he'd risked his life to save part of the ship during a hurricane.[2] He received a number of Good Conduct awards.

On the other hand though, early in his naval career, he spent the night in the brig several times for negative things he did (like slugging an officer in a club) while intoxicated. He also served time in the brig for breaking curfew. It was difficult to handle problems at home and be aboard ship at the same time.

One fact became very clear: Daddy was not mentally ill. He was not schizophrenic, as Mama had claimed. The only reference that comes close to the word *schizophrenia* is the notation on his medical file indicating that a Schiotz tonometer was used to measure whether or not he had glaucoma. He did not.[3] This was the page from his records that was shown to the jury to indicate Daddy was mentally ill. Why didn't they fully investigate his records? They would have found quite the opposite of what they were told by Mama. In fact, his records show he was not only physically and mentally healthy, but—to quote his commanding officer on Daddy's performance evaluation just a few years before his death—he was "an outstanding commissaryman in all respects."

The evaluation also notes, "No matter what the situation, he always handles his work capably and efficiently; he can always be counted on to get the job done with no supervision required. His unfailing cheerful personality enables him to get good results from those under him and to get along well with the rest of the crew. His military appearance is excellent. Written and spoken command of English are adequate. It has been a distinct pleasure to have [him] aboard."[4]

On his performance evaluation a year later, another commanding officer stated he "takes the initiative and effectively accomplishes every task assigned in an excellent manner. [His] military behavior is of the highest caliber. His sound judgment, thoroughness, and leadership qualities are evident in the execution of his assigned tasks. He has been instrumental in maintaining a high state of morale in the Division." [5]

On Daddy's final evaluation just prior to his retirement and transfer to Fleet Reserve, he received the highest marks possible. It reads, "[He, in his] assigned duties as watch captain, has been extremely effective and reliable; he willingly accepts responsibility and has high standards of military behavior. He possesses and effectively uses his ability to instill confidence in his men and inspires them to excel in all they do. His uniform is always impressive, smart, and worn with pride. [He] gets along exceptionally well with his shipmates. Both seniors and juniors."

This commander went on to say, "[His] military behavior is of the highest caliber and beyond reproach. He is meticulous in his appearance and sets an outstanding example for others. [His] ability to get along with others is reflected in the high morale of the galley."[6]

After a rocky start to his naval career, Daddy settled down and became an accomplished military serviceman. I am proud to be his daughter.

Indeed, Daddy never meant to harm us. Mama lied that night. Daddy was lying down in the car—not peering through the house windows—and rose when the sheriff's deputy arrived. Why did she say he was going to pick us off with a rifle, one by one? Because she never missed an opportunity to turn us against him.

When I think about sitting there that night, I no longer feel the fear of having my head blown off. It was a lie. The truth is that he was just as scared as we were—in fact, more so. He had reason to be scared; we did not. The truth set me free.

Through many counseling sessions, Paul taught me how to help myself. Now, any time I sense anxiety about anything, I seek the truth. Sometimes it is easy; sometimes it is not. If it gets to be too much for me, I stop the self-help process and make an appointment with Paul.

> For I know the thoughts that I think toward
> you, saith the LORD, thoughts of
> peace, and not of evil, to give you an expected end.
> —Jeremiah 29:11

11

"Father's Day is coming up, Daddy! Do you have plans for Sunday dinner?" Our son, Rob, had called his dad to invite us to a cookout at his house to celebrate the day. I offered to bring potato salad, a specialty of mine.

After church that Sunday, we headed over to Rob's house with healthy appetites and a large bowl of Southern potato salad. Rob was a wonderful cook at the grill and served up some beef and shrimp shish kebabs, which looked like they'd popped off the cover of *Bon Appétit*, and his wife served tasty side dishes to round out the meal. Great food and great company. We left there stuffed but happy and headed into the city to do some shopping. Anna wanted to go to a pet store to look at birds. Grant had Home Depot and Lowe's in mind. I was just along for the ride and didn't care where we went.

As we rode along, discussing possible purchases, a sour look crossed Grant's face.

"What's wrong?" I asked.

"Nothing," he replied.

I knew something was wrong, especially after he said *nothing* the way he did. I asked again.

He turned to me with tight lips. "We'll talk about it when we get home."

I felt like I had swallowed a bowling ball. Panic swelled inside me. I wanted to go home right then. I could not wait to find out the problem behind his discontent. What had I done? Or not done? He wouldn't say. He wouldn't discuss our problems in front of anyone, not even our daughter. I sat there with my hands in my lap, very afraid, looking out of the car window. I wanted to disappear, just vaporize into nothing.

They shopped, and I dragged behind them. At the pet store, Grant helped Anna pick out a nice bird while I gathered the bird necessities. Finished at last, we went home. I felt such a dread; I didn't even want to get out of the car.

At home, Grant expressed privately his disappointment that I allowed Anna to have a pet in the apartment without first letting him know. He doesn't like the noise and the mess that birds make.

"The mess is hers to clean up," I replied, "and the noise shouldn't be a problem. She lives in the apartment."

It turned out the bird wasn't the real issue; it was his not being informed. He said he would have liked to know she was getting a pet before she actually got one because a pet is a responsibility and could change the dynamics of our household. We should have discussed it. He felt she would care for the bird, but if she didn't, the responsibility would fall to him—that had happened with other animals she'd had. Grant was a Daniel Boone kind of guy, and animals and nature are important to him. He won't let an animal suffer needlessly from lack of care.

"I'm sorry I didn't talk to you about it. Please, please, please don't be mad." I was wringing my hands.

He looked at me oddly. I felt like a child. He spoke softly. "I'm not mad. I just wish we had talked it over first. Why are you falling apart?"

I went to my recliner, contemplating his question, while everyone else went to bed. As I sat there rocking, I pondered the scene in the car.

I remembered that when Grant had said, "We'll talk about it when we get home," his face had changed into Mama's.

On more than one occasion Mama had said, "I'll deal with you when we get home." Anytime she said that it knocked the air out of me because I knew "deal with you" meant the use of the folded extension cord.

Why did I react that way to my husband? He is good to me. We did go through some rough times early in our marriage. He had high blood pressure, and I had an anxiety disorder complicated by depression—a troubling set of circumstances to deal with for anyone. Sometimes we did fight, but it didn't go on too long. Our love for each other won out, and his doctors helped him get his blood pressure under control. My doctor tried to help me with my anxiety too, but the pills made me worse. We had to find another way. Grant and I together learned to cope with my fears. We learned to talk about everything. Communication is key. Now, years later, we have a loving, peaceful relationship.

So why had I reacted as I did? Authority. I have a great respect for authority. My husband is the head of our home, and though he is not a tyrant, I consider him the authority figure. I know he likes to be informed, and I didn't deliberately leave him out of the loop. It just never came up until we were on our way to the pet store.

I never deliberately disrespected Mama either. (No one in his right mind would do that.) But sometimes I messed up and paid dearly for it. I realized, sitting in my recliner in the dark, those mess-ups were normal for a kid. Maybe I was loud at the wrong time, or scuffled with a sibling, or ran through the house. We never knew when Mama would say, "I've had enough. You are getting a whipping for that." It could be the smallest thing, but she'd say it was "the straw that broke the camel's back." What were the other straws? And sometimes she whipped us all when one person "broke the camel's back."

I remembered our pleas as she pulled the cord out of the drawer. "Mama, ple-e-ease don't! We'll be good." We were already crying, and she hadn't even touched us. We sat in a row on the couch, our feet together and our hands in our laps, hoping our goodness would impress her. It didn't. When the cord came out, Mama never changed her mind.

In the recliner, the little girl in me cried.

Jesus spoke through my tears. *"You are human; you won't do everything perfectly. And you will make real mistakes. Learn from them. As a child, you were punished but not now. Focus on what you can learn from each mistake. That is how you grow."*

My husband got out of bed and came to the living room, looking for me. "Are you all right?" I told him about the whippings and how, in my mind, he was the authority figure, and I never wanted to disappoint him. "I understand. It's not the same, though. You are grown. And I'm not your Mama."

"I know." The adult me did know, but the little girl inside still shook. "But it still scares me to see disappointment on your face. I can't explain it. With Mama, a minor disappointment meant punishment. It was all she needed for the cord to come out. Sometimes she didn't even need that. Sometimes she whipped us on 'general principle'—just because she wanted to."

I remembered how she looked after she beat us. It was a workout. She'd be breathing hard, but she looked satisfied. "Mama seemed to feel better, almost refreshed, after beating us bloody. How is that good parenting? What were we supposed to learn from that?"

Heading back to the bedroom, shaking his head, Grant said, "It's not, and I have no clue."

After drinking a glass of milk, I was ready to turn in for the night, curled in the arms of my sweet husband. I felt certain I would deal with the day's events in my next session with Paul. Shaking my head,

I thought about the years I had spent in Paul's office already and wondered if I'd ever be totally free.

At the next session, I told Paul about my Father's Day meltdown; then we prayed. As soon as I closed my eyes, I felt the soothing peace of Jesus, and the memory opened up.

> Mama opened the desk drawer and pulled out the folded cord. As its only use was our punishment, the folds were permanent. She sent the two toddlers to their rooms. They ran. I knew this was about to get bad.
>
> Dean and I begged her not to whip us. As Mama pushed up the sleeves on her shirt, Dean gave up quickly and joined Lori and Wendy on the couch. Their feet were together, their hands folded in their laps—except for Lori, whose hands covered her mouth, her eyes wide with terror. I kept begging Mama until she told me to shut up and swung the cord at me. I joined the others on the couch.
>
> Mama took us, two at a time, into her bedroom. We cried waiting for our turn. Dean and Lori had to go first. I wanted to go first so I could get it over with. Dreading my turn and hearing the others' screams added to the torture.
>
> When Mama finished with them, they came out crying so hard they could hardly breathe. Dean was as broken as I'd ever seen him. Lori's face was pale; her lips were purple. Mama waved in Wendy, who was six, and me, twelve. As we walked into the bedroom, Wendy's blue eyes searched mine. She had no clue why this was happening. Even I didn't know who did

what to bring this on. It was probably me, though I wasn't sure. I watched Mama stripe Wendy's naked butt and legs and put my hands over my ears to muffle the screams.

I didn't dare close my eyes for fear she'd signal my turn to lean over the bed, and I wouldn't see it; then she'd hit me anywhere. I didn't want to be hit in the face. Gritting my teeth, I wanted to take that cord away from Mama and strangle her with it. If she ever sensed anger in us, though, she did her best to beat it out of us. I couldn't let my anger show that day.

Paul asked what negative emotion I felt.

"Anger and fear."

He asked if I would let Jesus take the anger away.

"Yes, in a minute." I wanted to feel the anger. It felt good to finally let it manifest instead of suppressing it. I wanted to see her as I'd imagined: choking, the cord wrapped around her throat. Wendy's questioning blue eyes and the raw, bulging purple and red stripes on her naked white butt fueled my anger. If I was at fault, why didn't Mama just whip me? Wendy's suffering hurt me far worse than the whipping I got that day.

Finally, the anger became too much to bear, and I said, "Yes, Jesus, please take the anger away." When the anger left, the fear remained. Mama's eyes—pale blue, cold, and vicious—contained no compassion, no mercy. That is why I didn't take the cord from her that day or any day.

Paul prayed.

The twelve year-old had said, *"I will survive this; tomorrow will come. Forget this. The worst is over. Block out the pain. I will look forward to the future."*

Now living in that future, I agreed. I did survive. Mama's authority no longer was valid. She could not punish us anymore.

I transferred Mama's authority to my husband on our wedding day because he became the one who took care of me. The little girl in me brought that past pain right into the marriage. Talk about baggage; I had plenty.

That little girl needed to be healed, reassured, and comforted. That is what Mama owed me but could never give me. In Paul's office, I forgave her, gave the debt to Jesus, and moved forward. He healed, reassured, and comforted me.

My relationship with Grant grew stronger. Our lives are governed by real love—unselfish love. I can depend on it and know he has my best interest at heart. He feels the same. I told him if another person tries to physically harm me, no matter who he or she is, I do not have to accept it or tolerate it. Grant said he'd better not hear of anyone trying to harm me. I laughed. He didn't. I love him.

I knew all of the fears wouldn't disappear overnight, but I was determined to work on conquering them day by day. Someone told me once that the word "fear" is an acronym for False Evidence Appearing Real. I learned in Paul Thompson's office to face the fear, search for the false evidence (the lie) causing it, and allow the truth to take its place. Sometimes the truth is as plain as the nose on my face; other times I have to search Scripture or pray for it. God is faithful, and the truth is revealed. It's like flipping on a light switch at midnight in a cabin deep in the woods. When the darkness (the lie) dissolves, so does the fear. So each time I feel a twinge of fear, I remind myself that its root is a lie. God reveals the truth one bit at a time, turning on the light and setting me free.

My oldest daughter ran barefoot into a sandspur patch when she was five years old. She cried out in pain. I pulled her up and looked at her feet. I had the heart-wrenching job of holding her in my lap and pulling out the sandspurs—too many to count—one at a time. That was the least painful for her and only way to make sure we removed them all, leaving no thorns in her feet. Some were deeper than others, but all of them hurt. She cried, and I comforted, snatching them out as quickly as possible to minimize pain.

I know how she felt.

A nightmare woke me up. The details escaped me, but the anxiety didn't. I didn't want to close my eyes again, so at four-thirty in the morning I was awake for the day. I planned ahead. Grant would soon be up getting up for work. I'd have his lunch ready. A load of towels would be in the washer or maybe in the dryer by then. I wouldn't have much rest, but I would get a jump-start on the chores for the day.

By six o'clock, my husband was on his way to work, and my running around like a white tornado, doing my chores, had not only satisfied my need for a clean house but also had relieved most of the anxiety, leaving me very hungry. While virtually inhaling pecan granola cereal soaked in cold milk, I studied my devotion open on the bed. "My grace is sufficient for thee, for my strength is made perfect in weakness" (2 Corinthians 12:9).

What is grace, really? In religious circles, it is one of those cliché words—like "saved" or "baptized." When I looked up the definition of grace, I found that it means "unearned favor."

Jesus favors me, and I didn't do a thing to earn it. Earn it? Who could earn it anyway? He is the Son of God. He doesn't have to favor anyone or anything. But He's different from any earthly prince or king. It didn't go to His head, being the Son of God. Loving and kind, He's passionate even about saving a scrawny, beat-up, little redheaded girl. Why? Because of who He is. I marvel still.

I looked up the rest of the words and translated the verse into everyday language. The truth in it lifted my spirits and cleansed me of the morning's anxiety. "My unearned favor is able to do whatever you need, because My power is brought to the highest degree in your lack of power."

In other words, though I don't deserve it, He favors me, and in my weakest moments, that favor turns into strength—His strength, not mine. It's a strength that can bring me through anything. He has proven this over and over to me. Good to know, too, because if I had to face these issues from the past by myself, Grant would need to check me into a mental health facility. Maybe that is why Dean is there. Though grace is a gift, free to all, it has to be accepted.

I sensed Jesus speak from deep in my spirit. *"Freely you have received; freely give."*

I knew that Scripture, but I wasn't sure how it fit into my present train of thought. *What?*

"You have been freely given grace. I've noticed you freely offering grace too."

What do You mean? I silently asked.

"By truly forgiving those who have wronged you and giving the debt to Me, you are extending favor to them."

Favor? Really? To be honest, I don't like the ones who hurt me, and I really don't like what they did. How is that favor?

"You are not required to like them, and you are not excusing what they did. You provide favor by releasing them from the offense, separating the sinner from the sin, and giving the sin debt to Me. I paid the debt for all sin, yours and theirs.

I thought of the Lord's Prayer I prayed every morning over my family and me. *Kind of like, 'Forgive us our debts, as we forgive our debtors'?*[7]

"Not kind of like, exactly like. Grace streams. It is meant to flow to you and through you. Those who have offended you don't deserve your favor, but you keep giving it. Just as our Father does for you."

Forgiveness is a big deal for me and for them. I thought about the verse earlier. His grace gave me the strength to forgive those who wronged me. *Thank you, Jesus.*

He smiled.

The dryer buzzed. As I went to get the towels, a song drifted through my mind. I began to sing it softly while pulling the towels into the basket. I have sung "Jesus Loves Me" since I learned it as a kid at that southern Georgia Baptist church, but never had the verse meant more to me than at that moment. I sang out, "They are weak, but He is strong."[8]

He is strong—stronger than my abuser. Since He loves me, and He's so strong, why have I had to suffer so much? I thought about the strength He gave me to forgive. I decided if I could have been spared all of that abuse I wouldn't have to forgive. An ounce of prevention is worth a pound of cure. Right? Couldn't He have prevented any of it? God is not afraid of my hard questions.

Actually, He did prevent some abuse. There were times when He told me to hide. I heard Him and did what He said. Not everyone does. God gave each of us the right to choose. Some of us choose the dark side. We live in a world where sinful people do sinful things, and it dawned on me that because of His love and by His power, He doesn't keep me from the world; He keeps me in it. People disobey, displease, and grieve Him, but He is still able to take care of His own. He. Keeps. Me.

My Lord never ceases to amaze me. No matter what life has thrown at me, His grace—that unearned favor—has kept me alive and sane. The latter, of course, is left to interpretation.

12

"There's something I need to tell you," I confessed to Paul.

"Okay." Paul smiled and waited for me to continue.

The last few years had been an emotional roller coaster. There had been great breakthrough highs followed by troubled lows. Then there were the joyful times, where I learned more about the love and care of God, and the confusing times, like on this day.

"It's about the drowning memory," I began. "As a weak little child, I needed the strong Savior. I know my Grandma prayed for me. I know Jesus loves me, and I know He has the power to do anything. Jesus should have been there, but He wasn't."

"And you are upset with Him about that?"

I nervously replied, "Yes, I am."

Nervous? How can a person actually say aloud that she is upset with the Son of God? It seemed presumptuous to me. I took a deep breath and explained that I really felt this way, and if I couldn't be honest with Jesus, who could I be honest with?

Paul agreed.

"Why was Jesus absent when Mama drowned me?" I asked. I described the entire memory again, piece by piece, and told Paul the only presence I felt was the guardian. He is not Jesus. I know the difference between the presence of Jesus and that of a guardian angel.

Paul replied, "Jesus, how do you respond to that?"

I closed my eyes and listened deeply.

Jesus said, *"I was there. I stayed in the background because God has a plan and a purpose for your life yet unfulfilled. If you'd known I was there, you would have wanted to stay with me. I couldn't let you, so I remained at a distance, overseeing your situation."*

Four- or five-year-old me, I am sure, would have clung to Him. Would it have saddened Him to turn me away? To send me back to an abusive home? Would I have begged to go with Him? To all of those questions, I think the answer is yes.

With Jesus, I have a relationship, and in relationships there are choices. That was the difference. The angel never offered a choice. (I don't think he gets to offer one.) He guided and protected me as I stared at my brother in the dark living room, traveled back to the bathroom, and zoomed in close to the dead little girl's face. Each scene just happened, without any thinking or decision making. The next thing I knew, I found myself in a dark room where I heard Mama yell at me to breathe.

Why didn't you stop Mama; keep her from drowning me? I asked Jesus.

He looked sad and knowing, as if He understood why I asked. *"There are certain rights and responsibilities given to parents. When she went beyond those, we had to step in. Many parents don't know how to care for or discipline their children the right way; they follow the pattern shown them as children. For you and many others ... tragic."*

Paul asked if the inner little girl felt calm and peaceful.

I asked the five-year-old, and when she looked at me, her face distorted. It looked awful. When I told Paul, he said there were still more memories she needed to open up and deal with.

By talking about the scene of the car tire by my face, the hot asphalt, and the smell of car exhaust, we tried to get that memory to open. Nothing. He said to ask my inner mind why I could not go there, and why the memory did not open up and flow. When I asked, the memory opened a small bit. I felt tremendous pain in my body. Then the memory closed again. Too much pain.

Paul asked Jesus to handle this.

Jesus told me I couldn't deal with the whole memory at one time. He would give me bits and pieces of it, like a jigsaw puzzle. When I was able to cope with each small piece, he would put all the pieces together to make the big picture.

I sat there, overwhelmed, with my entire childhood on my mind. "I can't handle this. It's just too much."

Paul said, "Jesus, what do you want Carly to know about that?"

Jesus spoke firmly. *"You have, you can, and you will."*

I chuckled. He'd cut to the chase. I also realized He was right. I certainly had. I guess I could. And I wanted to be anxiety-free, so I was willing.

He smiled and added softly, *"And I will help you."*

I knew He would. I immediately felt strengthened and ready to move forward.

I saw a window with a white painted frame. A black nail dotted the windowsill. I focused on the nail and let my mind float away.

I told Paul that when I suffered through a beating or some other painful experience as a child, I escaped by concentrating on one thing—anything—and let my mind go elsewhere until the physical suffering ended. That is how I survived.

I realized again I was sane only because of Jesus. For my entire life, my invisible friend, Jesus, had talked to me and helped me bear the suffering.

On the way home, I thought about the window frame and my focusing on the nail. It puzzled me. The pain I experienced at that time carried a separate and unusual mind-set, different from the pain of a beating. I felt something else, a confusing kind of pain. A million thoughts raced through my head. I concentrated on the memory. It opened up.

> My hands held onto the windowsill as I watched some kids my age playing outside. They held hands in a circle and danced around and around, singing. They were laughing and having a great time. Then they fell down all at once.
>
> I longed to go outside and have fun with them. Mama said I couldn't because she didn't want me to get dirty. When the kids ran out of my view, I realized something was happening to me that I didn't understand. I knew not to fight it, though, I didn't even cry. I'd been through this before. I focused on the nail and let my mind escape.

In the car, my chest hurt; I felt nauseated. Surely not ... oh, tell me that did not happen. Disgusted and appalled at what I knew, I couldn't wait to get home. As before, disbelief battled truth. Would I get any sleep tonight?

Lying in the quiet stillness that night, I saw again the black nail on the white windowsill. I convinced myself to let the memory unfold. I wanted to know the truth.

> I was standing at the front window of Mama and Daddy's bedroom. Outside, some kids were playing in a circle. They ran around and around singing, laughing, and then falling down. Others on the outskirts then took their places. I yearned to go outside and play with them. I knew I could play their game, I had seen those kids play it many times.
>
> Earlier, I had asked Mama if I could go outside. She'd said no; she didn't want me to get dirty. As I stood at the window,

the kids ran away. I realized something was happening to me that I didn't understand. It hurt, too. With my distraction gone, I became frantic, and looked for something else to focus on so I could let my mind drift to a different place away from the pain. A black nail in the white windowsill caught my eye. I concentrated all of my attention on it and stifled a cry. We were not allowed to cry. I planted my feet and continued to focus on the nail.

Grant heard me gasp and hold my breath. He reached out to me and asked me what was wrong. I couldn't speak. The realization of what had happened hurt more than I could bear. I almost called Paul right then. Finally, the tears came.

Grant knew it was something I'd remembered and told me that whatever happened would never happen again. I could be sure of that, he said. He held me tight. Again, disbelief fought truth, while anger and hate waited in the wings. Disbelief finally won. I fell asleep and dreamed.

While walking through the church annex on my way to the ladies' luncheon in the fellowship hall, I spotted a beaded-jewelry booth and stopped to look over the assortment, as beading was a hobby of mine.

As I perused the beads, a dark cloud outside caught my eye. I hurried to the window to see dark clouds swirling and strong winds whipping the trees. Debris flew everywhere. Stepping outside to get a better view, I noticed a funnel cloud. It was a blur at first but rapidly took form and headed toward the church.

A young girl, standing to my left, also watched the storm. We joined hands and found a place to hide until the funnel cloud passed. Black clouds with pelting rain persisted, and we hid again as another tornado tumbled by, heading toward the sunset. After it passed, I noticed all of the ladies were gone, including the lady with the bead booth.

Right away, another tornado, bigger than the others, barreled right for us. Grabbing the girl and Grandma (I don't know where she came from), we climbed into my car. Holding onto each other, we anchored ourselves just before the tornado tumbled the car like a tennis shoe in a washing machine. I closed my eyes.

When it stopped, the car sat upright but on the other side of the church parking lot. Grandma smiled; we were all fine. I got out of the car and made my way toward the church. From all directions people ran onto the church grounds to survey the damage. Tree limbs cluttered the ground everywhere, and the roof of the church showed some minor damage. One of the elders said we were fortunate to have survived that one. I looked to the right; there loomed another tornado on the horizon. Holding our collective breath, we watched it come closer, but then it turned and veered away from us. Everyone let out a sigh of relief.

Something from inside the church pulled at me. Unsure of the damage, I cautiously stepped inside the door at the back of the church and stood in front of a small oblong table. Glancing around the sanctuary, I sensed perfect peace. The room looked undisturbed, with everything in its place. The golden light coming through the ornate glass windows cast a comforting glow.

On the table a black velvet box rested on a white lace doily. I picked up the box and looked inside. There, in a tangled wad, lay several strands of pearls. My pearls. I gasped when I saw them.

Jesus stepped up from behind me and said, *"Look at them."*

I cried, "I know! They're ruined! I'll never be able to straighten out this mess!"

He repeated, *"Look at them, Carly, closely. Tell me what you see."*

I picked up the clump. "I see a mess. They're all twisted and tangled!"

He placed His hands under mine. I looked up at Him as He spoke. *"They're not dirty. They're not broken."*

I looked back at the pearls.
He said, *"They're just in disarray."*

By noon the next day, the ugliness of the abuse had overwhelmed me. I called Paul. "I cannot handle the truth," I sobbed. I shared the window-nail experience, and guilt attacked me. He asked me about the guilt. I told him about seeing Mama's angry face.

Later, in Paul's office ...

> I was six. I saw Mama's face. Angry, she told me if I told anybody the things she'd done, I'd be in trouble. She made me promise I would never tell, not ever. Then her face became pitiful, and she said if I told, people would take me away from her. She said I had to protect her. Right then, I made up my mind to protect her forever because I loved her.

Paul said, "Jesus, how do You respond to that?"
I waited. Nothing. I heard, saw, and felt nothing.
After a moment or two, Paul asked, "What's going on?"
"Nothing."
Then I saw a hallway. Jesus told me to relax. Several times during this session Jesus told me to relax. It was difficult.

> I was looking down the long hallway. I saw a half-open door at the end. The hallway was dim and stuffy, but the view beyond the door looked bright and airy. A young version of Mama stood behind me. I turned to her. She repeated some words I couldn't

understand and then mumbled, "Protect me, protect me." Over and over she said the same phrase.

Jesus spoke. *"Turn around, face the door, close your ears, and walk forward."*

I tried to do what He said, but I couldn't walk forward. Off to my left, I saw an old version of Mama, bent over in a wheelchair. She turned the chair sideways and refused to look at me.

Paul asked several times what these things meant to me. I had to answer, "I don't know." Jesus would have to explain most of this, for I had no idea.

Jesus said the young Mama behind me was not the real Mama; the one in the wheelchair was. I noticed I was tethered to the young Mama by a black cord with white writing on it that read, "Protect me, protect me."

Jesus instructed, *"You have to stop protecting her. God can't help her until she faces her pain. We love her. Untie the cord. Stop protecting her."*

I can't, I answered. *I don't want to hurt her!*

"You hurt Anna. You made her face the truth and come to Paul's office for counseling when she didn't want to. She screamed and cursed at you, but you made her do it anyway. And look at her now."

I told Paul everything as it was spoken. He asked, "What is the worst that can happen if you talk about it?"

Before I could speak, Jesus said, *"She'll be angry first and then sad."*

What? I was astounded. *I've been protecting her for fifty years so she wouldn't be sad?*

I told Paul about Mama's possible reactions to my discussion of the abuse. I also told him that I was through protecting her. No longer six years old or afraid, I felt determined to be emotionally healed.

I reached back and untied the cord. The young Mama folded up and faded away. The old Mama turned her wheelchair toward me. With lips parted to show clenched teeth and scowling eyes fixed on me, she snarled my name. Anger burned red-hot in her face.

Without fear, I looked straight at her and said, "Get over it, Mama," and turned to walk toward the door. Someone grabbed my hand. Lori. From close behind me, Grant, Vickie, Brent, Glenda, and the rest of those who had supported me stepped up and walked with me. My pastor, my children, and my friends kept walking. Every step I took, they took.

As I got closer to the door, my stomach knotted up. Anxiety grabbed me, and I stopped. I couldn't take another step.

"I don't understand," I said to Paul. "I can't go any further."
Paul said, "What is holding you back?"
"I have no idea."
"Search inside. What is your mind saying to you?"
"What if Mama says I'm lying?"

Jesus responded, *"The truth will overcome. The lies will be exposed. Why do you think you are in counseling now? The truth fought its way to the surface and has finally emerged. Truth will prevail."*

Iridescent Grace

The little girl in me protested. *I don't want to make her mad. I'm afraid of her.*

The Mama in the wheelchair smiled a wicked smile.

Jesus said, *"I won't let her hurt you again."*

Mama's face hardened. Angry, she turned her back to us again.

The little girl believed Him, but the adult was not so brave. Jesus again stepped into the fray with sword drawn, ready to stop any menacing foe.

I conceded. *Okay, I understand.*

I told Grant about the abuse when he got home from work that evening. He held me while I cried. Anger rose in him, but he managed it well. He mumbled something I probably didn't want to hear. I didn't want Mama to suffer or hurt. I just wanted this to be over.

I remembered trying to tell Grandma about it once, and she backhanded me, bloodying my lip. She said I should be ashamed of myself, telling tales about my mama like that. I never told her anything important again.

Days after my counseling appointment, I still couldn't stop thinking about the pain of it all.

I asked Jesus if I could just go ahead and forgive her and get past it.

He said, *"There's more."*

More? No! Please!

I didn't know if I could wait the five days for the next appointment. Either my mind or Jesus kept the memory from opening again outside of Paul's office. My imagination wreaked havoc with my logical thinking as I waited. I asked Jesus to make the lies dissolve so only the truth remained. I hoped all of it was a lie.

When the movie *Tangled* was released on DVD, I purchased it, as I love Disney animation. I told the girl at the register it was for my grandchildren. That was indeed true, but deep inside, I knew the little girl in me would grab a blanket and pile up on the sofa with them.

As we watched the movie, I was stirred by the themes presented. When the truth came out about Rapunzel (I won't spoil it here), I was blown away. How did she have the strength to stand up to Mother Gothel? Truth! She finally knew the truth. She knew there was something significant about the lights. Believing in the lights helped her find the truth. The truth set her free.

I also loved the part when the hero, Flynn Rider, rescued her. I could relate. My knight in shining armor had scooped me up after Daddy's death and protected me. *Tangled* instantly became my favorite movie of all time.

13

In Charleston in the early 1960s, Roy was Superman—or so he thought. The eight-year-old son of Mama's best friend, Josephine, came with her to our house most weekday afternoons. Dean was six and a half; I was a year younger. *Superman* on television, played by George Reeves, amazed us with feats of daring and strength at four o'clock each day. Usually about that time, Roy flew through the front door wearing a red towel or tablecloth tied around his neck. The red blur yelled, "Su-per-maaaan!" as he flew past us.

I thought Roy was stupid. He had big yellow teeth, usually filled with the leftovers from his afternoon snack. He ate all the time, constantly carrying a bag or package of something. We weren't allowed to ask for any of whatever he had, and he didn't offer to share, one of the reasons we hated him. He also had no manners, a virtue important to Mama. She told us she would never have a bunch of younguns like Roy, whom she'd be ashamed to take anywhere. I used my manners; it got ugly if I didn't.

Once, when I was about three years old, I sat at the kitchen table, eating with Mama and my brother. Manners were the farthest thing from my mind. I tried to come up with something to get my brother to laugh. I made faces, crossed my eyes, or did something strange with my food.

Mama said, "Carly, chew with your mouth closed." I did for a bit and then forgot again, laughing and talking to my brother, who rarely said anything at the table or anywhere. He looked at me with a sad face, knowing I would soon be in trouble.

She warned me again. The next time she caught me with my mouth open and full of food, she sent me from the table. No more supper. I climbed down, hungry and mad. I stuck my tongue out at her, turned to leave the room, and felt the tines of her fork sink deep into my back.

I screamed and ran, the fork flopping. I tried to get it out but couldn't reach it. Mama grabbed me and pulled it out, telling me how sorry she was. I didn't chew with my mouth open anymore.

After many appointments with Paul, I knew the drill. Sitting on the sofa, with my hands covering my eyes, I focused on Jesus and asked Him to help me get past this issue. I thought we would first go back to the windowsill and the nail, but we did not.

> Josephine and Roy arrived. Roy plopped down on the couch by Dean, barely missing Lori, who sat on the floor nearby. I growled at Roy as I steadied Lori, moving her farther away from his raggedy, used-to-be-black Keds high-tops. When I was sure she was out of the way, I went to ask Mama for a drink.
>
> Our afternoon snack was usually a glass of water. Since we weren't allowed in the kitchen without her, I had to catch Mama before she and Josephine went upstairs, "where it's quiet."
>
> As I reached the bottom step, they were laughing and talking, heading up the stairs, so I waited. Josephine became affectionate, but Mama brushed her off and, with a laugh, told her to wait until they got upstairs. Mama was always in a good

mood when Josephine was there. They didn't see me, and I was thirsty, so I followed them.

Upstairs, when they shut the bedroom door, I didn't know what to do. I heard them still laughing and talking, so I went into the bathroom and drank my fill from the sink. Loving the feel of the cold faucet and clean, clear water in my mouth, I played in the water for a bit.

When I came out of the bathroom, I didn't hear any talking or laughing. It was too quiet. I lingered by Mama's bedroom door, wondering if they'd gone downstairs, but I had neither heard nor seen them go by me. Besides, if Mama had seen me playing in the water, she'd have made her presence known. I also knew when the two of them went upstairs, they didn't usually come down for a long time, so I opened the bedroom door to see if they were in there. They were.

I stood there, stunned. Something was very wrong. Mama saw me and told me to come in. I couldn't move. She growled, *"Come here!"* through gritted teeth. I didn't want to go in, but I took a few steps. She said something about my being nosy and teaching me a lesson. They made me participate in their game, and when I tried to refuse, Mama got very angry, so I did what I was told. To say I was confused is an understatement. This was not Evil Mama or Good Mama. I didn't know who this Mama was.

There in Paul's office, several more similar memories ran through my mind; sometimes Dean was in them too. Lying on our parents' bed, Dean's tears streaked his face, and terror screamed from his eyes. His lips trembled as he held his breath. Neither of us dared to make a sound. I looked away from him. I was in my own torment.

I described only a small part of the memory to Paul. I felt too embarrassed. I said enough that he knew the situation. While talking, I had to remind myself to breathe. Though I knew that what I saw in the memories was real, disbelief continued to confront truth. I tried to ignore what I saw, to blur the details. I couldn't, and every painful detail came through in sharp, full, living color. Disbelief lost this round.

I felt so filthy.

Jesus said, *"Remember the pearls. You did what you were told to do. You had no choice. You two were the innocent ones. Remember the pearls."*

I pictured the pearls from my dream—clean and beautiful. I didn't feel that way at all.

I told myself it was not my fault, but I didn't believe it. If only I hadn't been a nosy little girl. Mama was convincing. I got what I deserved, but what about Dean? He never did anything wrong. I guess once I got pulled into the situation, he also had to be involved.

The adult me argued with the little girl me. No child ever deserved what happened to us. Mama was wrong! The adult won. I said it aloud, "Mama was wrong!"

Paul asked if I felt any unforgiveness there.

"Ya think?" I snapped.

"Sorry," he whispered. "Do you want to forgive her and give the debt to Jesus?"

It's all so ugly, I thought. *How could Mama do that to us? And the neighbor—she did her part.* I spotted the box of rocks. I couldn't carry the weight anymore.

"Yes," I answered Paul, "but first I have to figure out what she owes me."

"Okay."

"Innocence," I declared. "She owes me my innocence."

That's hopeless, I thought. *It's impossible to get innocence back. Once it's gone, that's it.* Like a robot, I took the second of the three large rocks from the box and gave it to Jesus, who laid it at the foot of the cross.

I waited for Jesus to speak, hungry for the words that would restore and strengthen me. He looked at the rock and then up at the cross but said nothing. My eyes locked on the rock, so heavy, dark, and ugly—a monument to my soiled childhood. I had carried it a long time. As I stared, drops of blood splattered on it. Innocence. Restored.

Fear not: for I have redeemed thee, I have called thee by thy name; thou art mine.

—Isaiah 43:1b

14

The next few days were a roller-coaster ride as the disturbing scenes played over in my mind whether I wanted them to or not. I tried to focus on the pearls; they were clean and whole but mixed up. I continued to remind myself of the restorative power in Jesus's blood and that I stood blameless for the abuse. With disbelief long gone, I knew all of it was real. Now anger, depression, and anxiety took turns wrestling with my psyche.

I refrained from telling Paul any of the details; they were just too personal and embarrassing. But how could I get rid of the anger and other negative emotions if I couldn't talk about them? I knew it was my decision. Paul never pressed for details, one of the reasons I liked going to him.

Paul listened well and knew just when to ask the right questions. I had been through therapy enough to know the drill, but when I made an effort to counsel myself about this, I found out just how important his role was.

I tried to talk to Jesus by myself about the worst parts of these memories, but then I became angry and couldn't control it. At one point I felt I was losing my mind, so I focused on something else and stopped attempting to be the counselor and the counselee at the same time. I knew Paul would help me work through each layer of emotions until I finally had them all resolved.

All resolved. How great that would be! Then I remembered the one huge rock still in my box. What could be as bad as drowning or sexual abuse? I didn't want to think about it, so I got busy cleaning and doing the laundry. Focus on something else; that's what I always did.

The cable guy knocked on the door. I let him in and went back to work tidying up the kitchen. After he left, I realized I had not had a rush of anxiety like I used to have when someone knocked on the door. My first thought used to be, *Who is here to kill me?* This time, however, I had no bad thoughts at all. I smiled, rather pleased. Progress ... I was making progress.

The next day I drove to the Florida Panhandle to spend the day with Lori. We had planned the visit several months before, not realizing at the time how desperately I would need a break.

The change in scenery was great, but the real benefit from the trip was seeing Lori—to look into her eyes and feel the connection. We had survived the same family, and she understood my difficulties, none of which I wanted to talk about that day.

When I arrived and she hugged me, the connection was there. I relaxed all over. I could have turned around and gone home, having received what I came for. That connection—knowing someone in the world knew exactly what I was feeling—was amazing and fulfilling.

Of course I stayed. We looked at some old family pictures I had, making light comments about how we'd gotten older and looked more like this relative or that one. We kept the conversation lighthearted; her family didn't need to hear about the drama so prevalent lately in my life. And on that day, I didn't feel a need to talk about it.

Moving spontaneously through the day, we did some shopping and had a nice lunch in an older part of town at a little café. Quiet and leisurely—it was just the kind of day I needed.

After we returned to their house, Lori's college-age daughter, Kelly, received a phone call from a friend that lit up her bright blue eyes and energized her normally easygoing manner.

She planned to be in a friend's wedding in a few days, and her chocolate-colored satin and taffeta gown needed an alteration. The person who called had originally planned to alter it but had fallen ill and couldn't do it. Kelly went into emergency mode. This did not mean panic for her; this meant action!

I told her I could do the job for her if she could locate a sewing machine closer than mine, which was several hours away. She called anyone she thought might have a machine but no luck. Finally, we went to town and bought one. Lori said she'd planned to get one soon anyway to do some quilting. Then we had to locate a special attachment, which turned up in a tiny mom-and-pop upholstery store in town. Lori and Kelly sure knew how to turn a problem into an adventure.

I thoroughly enjoyed working on that dress while my sister cooked supper. After supper I headed home, satisfied and comforted, delighted to have had a break from the struggling little girl inside, who on this day had kept quiet.

The next morning when I woke up, I thought about all of the times a voice that I now knew to be Jesus's had spoken encouragement to me as a child. I again remembered times He told me to tell Dean to go hide. I'd grabbed Lori and hid too, just before Josephine walked through the front door. Countless times He spared us from abuse.

During my devotional time, I asked Him why He'd spoken to me instead of Dean, who was older.

He said, *"You listened."*

One time when I was about six, Jesus visited with me on the front step of our apartment in Charleston, where I was getting ready to eat a peanut butter and jelly sandwich. I chose carefully where I sat. I refused to sit or step on a crack in the porch or sidewalk because Roy had said if I did, something bad would happen. I even heard some girls at school singing a jump-rope song about it, so that sealed it. It had to be true. I took all of this to heart and did whatever I could to avoid trouble.

There on the front steps, I would pull my sandwich apart and fold each part in half. I then had two sandwiches: one peanut butter and one jelly. I always ate the jelly first—it was my favorite—because after the peanut butter, I'd have to hurry to get a drink of water to dislodge much of it from the roof of my mouth. I couldn't go back inside with food in my hand, so logically, I ate the jelly sandwich first.

Everything had to be in twos or threes. It just had to be. I especially liked to see our feet when Dean, Lori, and I sat on the couch. Mama liked us to sit there, and all remained calm when I could see three sets of two feet. If Mama left the room, we tickled each other and laughed a lot. If she sat reading or watching television, though, we had to be quiet. I had a tough time with the quiet part, and that's why I usually ended up in the stairwell closet.

On one particular day, I remembered, Jesus sat on the front step with me and my sandwiches. I didn't know His name at the time, just that He was my invisible friend who helped me. I fell into my usual routine of "Today, nothing is real."

Some days I let part of what happened be real, but only if I saw Daddy or Grandma. Most days, I decided when I woke up in the morning that nothing was real, so when something bad happened, I wasn't afraid.

Jesus said, *"You can't keep doing this."*

What?

"Telling yourself things aren't real. Wandering off to another place when bad things happen."

Why not?

"One day you might not come back."

I'd thought about Daddy and how I wanted everything to be real when I was with him. I didn't know if I could keep myself from wandering, though, when bad stuff happened.

"I will help you," Jesus said.

Every day after that, when I told myself nothing was real, Jesus reminded me it was real and that I could face it. He eased me into it, letting me have every other day as unreal. Then I could have two real days and one unreal day, and so on. This became easier and easier to do. One day, I forgot all about the unreal days. We had moved to another city by then, and all of the very, very bad days faded like a nightmare.

Jesus also helped me to stop worrying about cracks in the floor or sidewalks. That was tough. I walked along jumping each crack. He told me to step on the next one, that nothing bad would happen because of it, but I didn't want to take the chance. I had enough bad stuff happening to me without bringing it on myself. Sometimes the pain had no other explanation. Finally, prodded by the kids at school telling me only stupid people believed they shouldn't step on cracks, I started listening to Jesus, and He proved to be right. When I walked home from school, I wanted to jump over the cracks, but I didn't. With the first crack I stepped on, I shook all over, convinced I had just set myself up for the next bit of trouble. Jesus calmed me and tried to assure me that when the next trouble came, it would have nothing to do with stepping on that crack. Still, I waited for the pain. When it came, relief followed. I'd paid the price for stepping on the crack.

Jesus convinced me to try an experiment. I stepped on every crack I could find to see if the number matched up to the amount of trouble that followed. If it did, I would probably die from it, which was fine with me. When everything went black, at least it would be over. Silence and peace always followed the black.

I was surprised that the amount of trouble did not match the number of stepped-on cracks. Roy was wrong. I didn't know why I'd believed him anyway.

I still got whippings I didn't understand and other pain that left me confused, but I concluded the sidewalk crack had nothing to do with it. By then, I was seven years old and smarter.

After that, Jesus worked on me about the twos and threes thing. That took a long time to stop, especially with Mama making me share everything. Anything good that came my way, Mama cut or broke into two or three pieces, and gave it to us to share. At least I got some of it. If it couldn't be shared or if it just appealed to me, it went into the garbage. I didn't get to keep it for myself. That only applied to me, however.

One Easter season, even though we didn't go to church, Mama decided we would each get a new outfit and go on a picnic. She let us pick the outfits from the catalog, and she ordered them. Excited, we talked for weeks about the new clothes.

Finally, a large package came. As the clothes came out of the package, everyone was jumping around and tearing the cellophane off the beautiful new outfits. I helped the younger ones with theirs. After removing all the outfits from the package, I noticed there were several outfits for the younger kids and something for Dean but nothing for me. Mama didn't even look surprised.

I was confused, "Where is mine?"

"They didn't have yours. It has to be reordered."

"What does that mean?"

"It will come in later." And she didn't want to hear another word about it.

I cried in silence. Somehow I knew. My new outfit would never come in. Not ever.

On the day of the picnic, I begged Mama to let me wear one of the younger girls' outfits. They had two or three each—I had counted them. Twos and threes had always been good to me. Why couldn't the younger girls share? She kept telling me I was too big. I begged her to at least let me try. I didn't want to be the only one on the picnic wearing old clothes. She finally said I could try.

At the picnic, the Capri pants I had stuffed my behind into split at the seam, and I was so embarrassed. Mama reminded me that she'd told me that would happen, and she made me wear them like that for the rest of the day. I told Lori I was sorry I'd torn her new outfit. She said it was okay; she had other new stuff. I still felt terrible and decided twos and threes were not good. I was done with them forever.

15

My next visit with Paul went quite well. We dealt with most of the issues entrenched in the sexual abuse—helplessness, hopelessness, and disrespect. As a child, when I tried to tell Grandma about it, her reaction let me know I had only a slight chance of being believed. I thought the abuse would go on forever, that it was to be my life. A memory opened in Paul's office that revealed one of the times I had found a faithful ear in Daddy.

Daddy had a shift change and began to come home at five or so in the afternoon. We kids loved that because we got to be with him more. He laughed and hugged and held us in his lap every day. I was stronger than Dean and bigger than Lori, so I claimed his lap first. I wasn't trying to be rude to them; I just got there faster. He made me share his attention, though, and when someone else filled his lap, I lingered close by.

I loved everything about him. Handsome, with true-blue eyes and dark, almost black hair, he had a thin build and average height. I saw him as a hero in his naval uniform. His voice was deep, and his laugh pure and infectious. I loved the way he smelled too—a perfect combination of hair oil, galley food, coffee, and Camel cigarettes.

> While Daddy was watching TV, I climbed into his lap but couldn't sit still because I hurt. Daddy asked me why. I told

him as the TV droned in the background. His mouth dropped open and his hand tightened on my shoulder. I pressed my face against him, waiting for the scolding. He didn't. I searched his eyes. He didn't understand and wanted to know more, his whole body focusing on my every word. I told him about Mama and Josephine, even about what they did to Dean. Daddy became very angry and stood me on my feet on his way to the kitchen, where Mama worked to get supper ready.

I crept to the edge of the room, hidden from view, and listened. Daddy asked Mama about what I had told him. At first she denied it, but then she told him if he would come home more often she wouldn't have to find entertainment. He slammed his hand on the table and told her Josephine was forbidden to come to our house anymore.

Mama started crying and said she understood.

He shouted, "I mean it!" He started to turn away but then turned back and said, "And you better not touch her for telling me either!"

When he walked out by me, I watched Mama. She sat down at the kitchen table and sobbed, her shoulders shaking.

I hid for a while.

Neither Josephine nor Roy came to our house again. The sexual abuse stopped, but the emotional damage was done. No matter how many times I told them I didn't want to do something, Mama made me do it anyway. Soon, I quit saying I didn't want to and just did it. My will was broken, and from then on, I did whatever I was told to do, with no back-talk and few questions.

Then Jesus reminded me that my will, God-given to me at birth, was a part of who I am. He said if I didn't want to do, say, or be something,

I shouldn't. I could choose. No longer a helpless child, I could make choices about myself and expect those choices to be respected.

Knowing there were inherent consequences for my choices, I always tried to make decisions that promoted life and pleased God. That is why I chose to forgive—every time. Concerning Mama and Josephine, all is forgiven. The debt is cleared. Jesus restored to me all they had taken.

The sexual abuse issue was at rest for the moment, but I looked for the next memory to open. I saw the car tire, smelled the exhaust, and felt the hot asphalt burning against my face. Some new pieces of the scene opened up.

> Blood trickled out of my right ear onto the asphalt. The extreme pain in my upper body accompanied an exploding headache. I couldn't move anything but my eyes. Some people were gathering around Mama, who stood somewhere behind my head. I couldn't see her, but I could hear people, including her, talking. One lady had a high-pitched voice. She talked fast and had more to say than anyone.
>
> Everything went black: no light, no sounds, and no smells. Then, clouds were all around me. I flew upward through the clouds, again escorted by my guardian angel.

I have never seen him, but I feel him. It's similar to someone being in the room with you and your back is to him. You know he is there without seeing or hearing him.

> I had no idea where we were going, but I was in a hurry to get there. I wanted to be far, far away from what was below.
>
> Over to my right, just ahead, I saw the corner of a large structure made of glass sticking out of the clouds. The glass

reflected the gold and pinks of the sunset far in the distance. It was so beautiful. I headed straight for the bright-colored structure, hungry to know more about it.

Abruptly, I stopped, turned, and looked down through the clouds, back toward the scene at the country store below. I knew we had to go back. No one asked or told me. I just knew. The beautiful structure, whatever it was, would have to wait.

The memory closed. I had not shared everything with Paul. Questions bombarded my mind. *Had my imagination interfered somehow? Too bizarre. Beautiful glass buildings? Please. When would this nut-case roller-coaster ride end?*

I told Paul I couldn't deal with any more.

"Okay," he said, and I'm sure he sensed my concern. As I left, he told me to call him if I needed him. I mumbled, "Uh-huh," and hurried through the door.

Going home, I didn't even play my usual calm-down music. I just wanted quiet. I prayed for truth. How much of this session was truth, and how much was imagination? Paul told me earlier that imagination is erratic, but truth remains consistent. I decided right then that before I would tell anyone about this, I would give it time to settle, so imagination could fall away and truth would remain.

The next morning, I woke up to a memory.

I heard Mama say, "I never wanted her anyway." My little-girl heart broke.

The other lady with the high-pitched voice said, "How can you say that? She's your child!"

I knew then why I'd wanted to leave the scene and go far, far away.

I asked Jesus why I had to turn around in the clouds and come back. He said, *"Your daddy pleaded for your life."*

As the light of dawn began to show through the curtains, I sobbed. Daddy had come through again. Why would he do that? Why didn't he just let me go? He loved me; that's why. But where was he? I hadn't heard him. Did he go into the store to call for help?

A couple of days later, I awakened before dawn, remembering what Mama and Daddy were fighting about in the car. I closed my eyes, relaxed, and let the entire scene play out.

We were coming back from a family picnic. Daddy drove along at a leisurely speed. Dean and I rode in the backseat, while Mama, holding tiny infant Lori, rode in the passenger seat in front of me. We cruised peacefully along, until Daddy told Mama he had to go back aboard ship. I was disappointed; Mama erupted.

"You're gone all the time!" Mama yelled. "You're never around to help with these kids."

"It's my job," he replied. "It puts food on the table and clothes on our backs."

"Day in and day out I have to take care of these kids, and I'm sick of it. I never have any fun! When you leave to go back to the ship, I'm going to give the kids away."

Daddy argued with her, his voice getting louder with each word, "That is the same way I grew up! With a mother who only thought about herself!" Then, softening his tone, he said, "Nobody wanted us. At least we were older. These kids are just babies. You can't do that."

"I will throw this baby out the window right now!" she screamed, reaching for the handle to roll the window down. "I'll get rid of them all and go back to my life before kids!"

Daddy's mouth fell open as he stared at her. I heard the window crack open and watched the opening get bigger and bigger.

I couldn't stand it. Lori was too small. I yearned for Mama to want us. It crushed me that she didn't. Daddy wanted us, but he couldn't be with us. He had to work so we could have food to eat and clothes to wear. I'd heard him say that before. The pain on his face hurt me. Mama, so cold and mean, kept rolling the window down.

Daddy believed her and began to slow down the car. It was too much for me. If Lori was going out the window, I'd be there to help her. I opened the car door to jump out.

The memory closed as I grabbed the box of tissues by the bed. I knew the tears would continue to flow for hours. My husband held me. I told him what I remembered. He assured me he wanted me and that God did too.

I knew what Paul would have said right then if I'd been sitting in his office. "Jesus, what do want Carly to know about this?" So I asked Him myself.

Jesus said, *"Your mama was a very sick woman. She didn't know the value of the family she had."*

My husband spoke up and said what he thought was obvious, "She didn't give you away. You all still lived with her until we married."

While he held me, I told him about a memory that had opened at church a year earlier when I prayed about the fear of abandonment I had. Not buried too deeply, this memory didn't contain anger, hate, or unforgiveness. It detailed the nervous breakdown Mama had had after

Daddy went back aboard ship another time. We were distributed among the neighbors, and thinking of it at that point, I was convinced Mama had succeeded in her plan to get rid of us.

I was five. The naval hospital ambulance pulled up in front of the apartments. Dean and I were on the front porch, looking through our screen door at the commotion inside. We had been pulled out of the apartment by neighbors who came when they heard Mama screaming. The neighbors went inside and tried to talk to her, but she wouldn't or couldn't stop screaming.

When the three men dressed in white uniforms with black shoes came out with Mama, she was wrapped up tight, from her shoulders to her hips, in a white thing with silver buckles on it. Dean stayed on the step, but I watched every move they made, running around to the back of the ambulance as they put her in it. She looked and sounded awful. Her face, red and swollen, was covered with tears and saliva. Her hair was messy, all out of place. Some of it was wet. Though she still screamed, her scratchy voice could barely make a sound. I kept asking them what was wrong with her, but everyone ignored me.

When they closed the back doors, got in the ambulance, and left, Josephine took Dean's hand and comforted him as they walked to her apartment. The neighbor who lived on the other side of us talked baby talk to Lori, cradling her in her arms as she ambled a couple of doors down to her place. I was left on the sidewalk alone.

When the ambulance drove completely out of sight, I walked over and sat on our front step. I decided then and there that I would survive. I knew where to find peanut butter, jelly, and bread. I could drink water. I didn't cry; I couldn't. There was too much to think about.

In a few minutes, the neighbor who had Lori came back for me. She led me by the hand to her house where, later that day, a beautiful lady with auburn hair took me home with her.

I was in the care of that family of three—four, including the dog—for several weeks. On the first day, any time they asked me a question, only one word came out: "Mama." I said it only a time or two. It was all I could manage. After that, I could not speak at all. My mouth seemed to be locked by the pain in my chest and the hollowness in the pit of my stomach.

I had never had a pet, so their little dog frightened me. They chained it to the clothesline pole, so it couldn't jump on me. The woman's ten-year-old son tried to get me to pet their dog. I refused every time, balling my fists and crossing my arms. He was gentle and never forced me. I liked him and his mother. She was also very gentle. I'd never been in a home so nice or so clean and uncluttered. She was a great cook, but there were some foods I'd never seen before. I didn't eat much.

The lady also took great care in my grooming. She brushed my short-cropped red hair every morning and night. Hers was nearly the same color as mine but long and beautiful. She took it down and brushed it every night too. I'd never met anyone like her. She was like a grown-up princess.

She always made sure I took a bath. She'd get it ready and then tell me she'd be back in a little while. It was the first time I'd ever taken bubble baths. Washing my hair was another thing entirely. She was careful to keep my head out of the water, rinsing the shampoo out by pouring water over my hair while I lifted my chin. She gave me a folded dry washcloth to hold on my forehead so the water wouldn't get in my eyes.

She bought me new clothes to wear because I only had the clothes I was wearing on the day Mama left, and the lady didn't like them. The new clothes fit right and smelled funny until after she washed them.

I got to sleep in her beautiful purple bedroom with her. I stared at the tiny purple lamps on each end of her dresser, marveling at them.

I had never seen anything so pretty. She didn't turn them off at night either. I was scared of the dark.

The purple-and-gold flowered bedspread was warm and comfortable. The bed felt even softer than Mama and Daddy's. After I wet the bed the first night, she took me to the bathroom in the middle of the night, every night.

I would have wanted to stay there if my family could have been there with me. I missed Mama and Daddy, Dean, and Lori too. I wondered if I would ever see any of them again. I was sad the whole time.

When the ten-year-old boy's daddy came home, he had on a naval uniform with gold things on the shoulder. His hat looked different from Daddy's. He looked important. I thought he didn't like me. His wife asked him about keeping me, and he said he didn't think it was a good idea; I had too many problems. He said, "She can't even talk, for crying out loud!" He had been standing there when they tried to get me to talk the day before.

The boy and his mom said they'd take me to the grocery store and buy me anything to eat if I'd just tell them what I wanted.

"Cookies, or candy, or anything," the son said.

I just stared at them. They already fed me better than I'd ever been fed, except at Grandma's house. All I wanted was my mama.

One morning, the lady told me to gather up my things; I was going home. As she helped me with my clothes and the toys they'd bought me, she said Mama felt better, and we would meet her at our house. The news sank in, and I got excited. I asked her if Dean and Lori would be there too. She grabbed me and hugged me tight, saying, "Yes, yes!" She smelled good. I couldn't wait to see Mama and my brother and sister. I was happy again.

This woman was a warm and loving person, but she wasn't my mama. I didn't belong to her. Belonging mattered. As bad as Mama treated me, she was still the center of my universe. After the lady with the auburn hair took me back to my family, I never saw her again. She had been good to me, and I wish now that I could thank her.

Mama's homecoming was wonderful. As soon as I got out of the lady's car, I ran with my arms wide open to Mama, who held Lori close. Dean tried to put his arms around us all. Grandma laughed. I couldn't stop hugging everybody. Mama laughed too. She hugged and kissed us. I really thought she loved us.

While Grandma stayed with us, life was good. The apartment smelled clean all the time. Every day, she cooked lots of food for us. She always woke up before we did and had food cooking when we got up—eggs and bacon or sausage, usually, like Daddy did on the days he was home. At lunchtime we ate stew meat and potatoes or sometimes beans and rice, along with Grandma's specialty, collard greens. Grandma also cooked the best chicken and rice in the world. Mama and Grandma talked and laughed every day in the kitchen. They hugged a lot too. Then, after a few weeks, Grandma went home, and Mama went downhill fast. Nothing had changed; the old Mama was back.

16

"How can a Mama just discard her child?" I asked my husband. Between appointments with Paul, I tried to go about my daily routine, but this time I struggled with being wanted. Back then, it seemed there were people who wanted us. Mama just wasn't one of them. "What awful thing had I done to earn her rejection?"

Grant comforted me. "No child deserves what you've been through. I don't care how many rules she's broken or what kind of little scoundrel she is. I am sure you weren't a scoundrel."

I chuckled. I probably had been. "You know, bright red hair and pale skin looks unappealing. Was I so ugly even my own mother couldn't love me?"

"Not the pictures I've seen," Grant said. "And you certainly aren't now."

"You're supposed to say that."

"It's not you. You are not the problem. I don't believe you ever were the problem."

That evening, while Grant watched his favorite TV show in the living room, I climbed into bed. Sitting with my knees on my chest and pulling the cover over my head, I cried aloud, begging Mama not to give us away.

From deep within, the words poured out into the darkness. I needed to get them out of me—words I'd wanted to say that day in the car after the picnic but couldn't for the pain in my heart. I found myself wanting to tell her how perfect I would be, reciting the list of good things I could do to impress her. I then realized my life had been a never-ending endeavor to be perfect and please her. I felt worthless because I had failed miserably. I wept until I had no tears left.

Later on, Grant came to bed, and as he slept peacefully, I remembered Mama taking us to the grocery store. It wasn't something she did often. Taking six kids anywhere was a hassle, so I worried the whole time that she planned to leave us there and never return.

I recalled not long ago experiencing anxiety when my husband left me in the grocery section at Walmart to go to the sporting goods department. As I watched him walk away, I stifled the urge to chase after him and grab his hand. *What is wrong with me?* I'd thought, shaking it off.

Another time, I couldn't shake it off, and before I had a full-blown anxiety attack, I went to Sporting Goods and shopped with him. He gave me a funny lock and wanted to know why I was tagging along with him. I just shrugged and stayed with him. I wasn't sure if I was afraid of the people, or the store, or what. *What a fruitcake*, I thought.

Lying there beside Grant that night, I realized I was afraid of being unwanted, of being left somewhere because I wasn't valuable enough to be taken home and loved. I cuddled up next to his lightly snoring body, so glad he had taken me home many years ago and continued to love me.

Mama told us repeatedly as we were growing up that her kids had to be perfect. There were so many rules, perfection proved difficult to achieve. Mama didn't let us play outside until we started school. She said she didn't want us to get dirty.

I tried to be perfect, but I couldn't be. I wanted to be loud. I wanted to be rowdy. I wanted to play outside and get dirty.

Once when Daddy was overseas, he wrote to Mama, telling her we needed to get out of the house more; we needed to go outside and play. We were very pale. Mama dressed us up and took us outside. She took pictures of us and then took us back inside. She sent the pictures to Daddy. Of course that wasn't what he meant.

One afternoon I snuck out of the house and climbed in the trash bin—a Dumpster—to hide. I knew Mama would never look for me there. Luckily, it was empty, except for a few pieces of food and a couple of cardboard boxes. It smelled nasty, but I needed a place to hide. If Mama caught me outside, the trouble I'd be in trumped the smell. I sat on one of the cardboard pieces, excited to be out of our house and hidden away from her.

After a few minutes, the scene of her catching me there and rubbing some of that nasty food in my face as punishment dimmed the excitement, so I climbed out and snuck back in the house. What an adventure.

No, I am not perfect, but who is? I guess I just didn't match what she wanted. I pictured the puppy at the pet store that everyone looked at and moved on. If she'd been allowed to choose, obviously she wouldn't have picked me.

I invited Jesus to join me in my wallow. *I have spent my whole life trying to find something I could do or be that Mama would find valuable and inspire her to want me.*

He responded, *"You are valuable simply because you exist. Nothing can be done to earn love. Stop 'doing' to please people and just 'be.'"*

I don't feel valuable enough to just be. I feel I have to earn my value, and where Mama's concerned, that's difficult—not impossible but difficult.

I thought about a couple of times I had earned value in her eyes.

When I was in college, I wrote an essay about the importance of reading aloud to children. I used Mama reading to us as an example. I detailed how she would pull us all together around her on the couch and read the story with animation and enthusiasm. I explained in the paper how important it is to show children that when those individual symbols were put in a certain order on the page, they represented knowledge and ideas to explore. Whole new worlds could be visited by deciphering the symbols on a page in a book. I gave examples of books Mama had read to us and explained that because of that, I'd grown up to love and benefit from the written word.

I received an A on the essay and positive comments from my professor. He noted I had succeeded in proving that reading to children benefits them as independent readers later in life.

After my professor returned the paper to me, I showed it to Mama. She was pleased I had honored her so. I felt good about pleasing her. It filled a spot in my heart.

Afterward, something nagged at me. I read through the paper several times, asking God why my soul was troubled. I mentioned to Lori what I had written, and she said she didn't remember a single time when Mama read to us. Not once. After consideration, I realized she was right.

The Mama in my essay was me. I read to my kids that way. I love books, and because I love my children, I wanted them to appreciate the written word from an early age and receive the life lessons found in the stories. I took great pleasure in reading to them and seeing their eyes brighten when the character achieved a goal or experienced a happy moment. Mama loved books too, but she didn't love us. She read only to herself.

Why had I portrayed her as a caring Mama who took time to nurture her children with life lessons from books? Two reasons: I wanted to have a mother like that, and I wanted to please her. Both of these reasons gave my life value.

Grant stirred, and I wondered if I had been thinking out loud. He drifted back to sleep, one arm over my waist. I was so thankful this man valued me for me. Since I had his love, why did I need a mother's love? Because it's a different kind of love—a love I was supposed to have when I was born. There was a place for it in my very core. When it wasn't there naturally, and I was reminded of that fact almost daily, what then?

As I lay there, I thought again about the college essay and wondered how many other times I had shoved the truth into a corner and believed a lie to feed my need to be loved by a good mother?

How many times was a memory going to emerge and bring to light some poignant truth from my past? All I knew was that more truth emerged every day, and I must walk in it. The more I allowed the memories to flow, the more truth I found, so I decided to let the memories emerge no matter the content.

Mama didn't like anything about me except school. I remembered how proud she looked when I first read aloud to her from my first-grade book. So I excelled at school. Reading, writing, and math came easy. I became the perfect student, doing everything my teacher asked. (I also loved school because I felt safe there.) Mama spoke proudly to her friends and relatives about my progress at school, so school became my shot at perfection and my escape.

Reading also became an escape. As a second-grader, my favorite book was *Thumbelina*. It is a story about a woman who longed for a child of her own but for some reason had none. Someone gave her a special seed. After she planted it, a flower grew. When the petals opened, a tiny sleeping baby lay curled up inside. She loved this little baby more than life itself. I pretended to be that tiny babe and imagined how great it would be to have a mother like that. I even pretended my mother loved me that much.

More memories brought more tears. I let them both flow.

Another favorite book of mine was *The Five Chinese Brothers.* Each of the brothers could defy death in some way. One could hold the sea in his mouth; another could stretch his legs as long as needed. Neither of these could drown. Another brother could not be burned, and still another had a neck of iron. The fifth could hold his breath forever. How marvelous. I wished to be all five at once.

As a sixth-grader, my favorite book told of the ingenious ways a young fellow named Jack outsmarted his would-be destroyer every time. The book, *Jack Tales,* made me laugh and reminded me that with some smarts and a sense of humor, one could survive.

I loved books, and I loved school.

Lying there after midnight, I realized I still did. I wanted my students to excel and feel safe. I wondered how many of them felt unwanted by their parents. I didn't know of any. Would they tell me? Eighth-graders are too old for *Thumbelina,* but they were not too old to be told they are valuable. Some might even be dealing with such horrors that the *Five Chinese Brothers* or *Jack Tales* could comfort them, as they did me. Had my teachers known? Did those books find their way into my hands purely by accident or by design?

More questions. What kind of teacher was I? Did I care enough about the student who had a home life from the pit? Yes, I did—but what was I doing about it? Were there books in my classroom that addressed life's down side, while pointing to love's up side, giving my students the shot of self-esteem and encouragement they needed? Yes. Were there books that showed courage and strength in the face of terrible circumstances? Yes, there were. Would my students connect with the characters and learn from the story? I could only hope.

Thank you, all of my teachers through the early years, for giving me courage and hope through stories, I thought. *Maybe that is why I became a teacher. I wanted to be like each of you.*

My pity party had transformed into a flood of gratitude.

Nestling down into the covers next to Grant, I finally realized that though I wasn't perfect and never would be, there were some folks along the way who valued me enough to teach me to read, write, and work with numbers. Thank God for them. As usual, Jesus was right; I did have value simply because I existed. Hadn't my teachers valued me just because I warmed a desk in their classrooms? Did I value my students? Yes, every single one of them, even the obnoxious ones. They were that way for a reason. I couldn't be their mama, but I could be someone who appreciated them. As the years go by, I might not remember each name, but each one will always have a place in my heart.

I glanced at the clock: 2:17. The alarm would go off at 5:20. What a night.

When I awoke with the alarm, I was still tired, and the emptiness of knowing my mama didn't want me returned. Shoving it aside, I washed my face, got my husband off to work, and started my day as usual, with Scripture and prayer. My devotional Scripture read, "Can a woman forget her sucking child, that she should not have compassion on the son of her womb? Yea, they may forget, yet will I not forget thee" (Isaiah 49:15). What timing! That livened me up.

I knew the Scripture referred to God's relationship with Israel, but something stirred deep within me as I read on. "Behold, I have graven thee on the palms of my hands; thy walls are continually before me. Thy children shall make haste; thy destroyers and those that made thee waste shall go forth of thee. Lift up thine eyes round about, and behold: all these gather themselves together, and come to thee. As I live, saith the LORD, thou shalt surely clothe thee with them all, as with an ornament, and bind them on thee, as a bride doeth" (Isaiah 49:16–18).

I am written on the palm of God's hands. Is that like carrying my picture in His wallet? I can't even begin to explain my excitement and the significance of this Scripture at that moment. When all the hurts in my childhood hurried back to me, I would wear them like jewelry. Did that mean I would own the hurt instead of the hurt owning me? Yes, it seemed so. And by the way, most brides wear pearls, don't they?

17

The following Friday, I drove to Paul's office by myself. On the way I thought about the memory of the whitewall tire. Again, I heard Mama's voice say, "I never wanted her anyway." My chest tightened, and I could hardly breathe. I was all too familiar with the symptoms of a panic attack and knew I had to focus my mind elsewhere, or I would be unable to drive. As the tingling in my fingers worsened and my chest and throat grew tighter, I begged Jesus to help me. I was fading into the gray, becoming invisible. My greatest hurt in that moment was that my value was zero. I was worth nothing and better off dead.

I hit the button for the radio. Loud music of any kind would do. I needed something, anything, to distract me from the emotional pain that seized my heart and head. The empty, worthless feeling was consuming me. With still more than an hour to drive, I wished I had asked Anna to come with me.

Though the battle surged, I braced myself, determined to stay the course instead of turning around and going home. The thought of giving in harassed me, but I continued to fight. Soothing sounds from the radio filled the car. Trying to keep from hyperventilating, I slowed my breathing and pulled the car over to the side of the highway. *Breathe in ... slowly. Breathe out ... Listen to the music. Focus on the words.*

The lyrics made faith sound so easy. I wanted to scream. *Praying and believing are not easy, especially when anxiety is eating you up. I'm* tired of fighting an enemy I can't see, who sneaks up and grips my mind. Refocus ... Listen to the lyrics.

I turned up the volume. The singer suggested a bright new day is on the horizon. Jesus did say to me at the beginning of several sessions, "Your future is bright," so this gray darkness had to end at some point. Another singer's voice, loving and soft, joined in the song, suggesting I let go of the fear.

Jesus, I don't even know what this fear is. If I did, I wouldn't be freaking out on the side of the highway!

The song played on. When I heard lyrics that told of all hope having vanished, I felt a connection. Then the singer, as if he were Jesus, spoke to my heart. "I'm here ... I'll never leave you. I'm your Savior," and I understood. I found the one piece of truth I needed, which dispelled the lie that caused this anxiety attack. I needed someone to want me, to value me. I needed to matter to someone. And that someone had to be more than a teacher or a friend who valued my existence only in certain circumstances. I needed someone to love me, good or bad, sweet or sour, quiet or loud. I needed someone to love me because I belonged to him or her. I felt like a lost child, looking for her father's hand to hold. When the lyrics said, "I'm your Savior," I believed.

He's my Savior. I matter to Him.

As the tears fell, I yearned for Daddy to be sitting right there by me in the car.

Jesus, I wish I had Daddy's hand to hold. If he could be here with me right now, he'd be an eighty-year-old shriveled-up prune, but I don't care. He'd still hold my hand. He wanted me. Never once did he reject me or my affection for him. He showed me in those moments what it meant to belong to someone.

Reaching out, Jesus assured me He would hold my hand in Daddy's place. I placed my hand in His.

Through prayer, the music, and my stress-releasing sobs, I relaxed. As the chorus played through again, I let it sink in.

Jesus will hold my hand in Daddy's place. I am valuable to both of them. Through every pain, from the beginning of my miserable life to now, I cried out to Jesus, and He heard. I matter to Him. He is my Savior.

When the song ended, I sang the important words to myself. "I matter to someone. I'm not invisible." The truth restored, I pulled back out onto the highway and drove the rest of the way, reminding myself that behind every fear is a lie, and no matter how long it takes, or what lie blindsides me, I will work through the process. I will get rid of the fears.

In Paul's office, I related the trip's events. He expressed concern, but I told him to relax; I'd dealt with anxiety many times (though not so much while driving).

"We need to get to the bottom of the anxiety," Paul said, "and get rid of it for good."

I agreed. Getting rid of all of my fears—and I had many—was something I prayed for daily.

When memories opened up in Paul's office, I knew any emotion could and would be dealt with properly. Ready to get this memory to the calm and peaceful stage, I silenced my phone, grabbed the box of tissues, and settled on the sofa. I never knew how long or how deep the session would go, so I prepared myself for anything. Or so I thought.

Paul prayed and reminded me to tell him everything I saw, felt, thought, or heard. The memory of the car opened up. It started with the argument and proceeded to the part where I opened the car door. Nothing changed from what I'd previously seen—but this time, it continued …

> Something caught my clothes, and I hung halfway out of the car. The door slammed into me pinning me between the door and the doorframe as Daddy sped up and swerved to the right into

a parking area. When he straightened and slowed the car, the door flung open again. This time, I fell all the way out, head and shoulder first, slamming onto the asphalt.

Coming to, I smelled the car exhaust and felt the asphalt hot against my face. When I opened my eyes, I saw only the whitewall tire. Struggling to breathe, I couldn't move. Any attempt to move caused excruciating pain in my upper body. I felt numb below my waist. Blood trickled out of my right ear. My huge head pounded.

Behind my head, people were talking. A lady with a high-pitched voice said, "Give me the baby. You go and see about her. She is badly hurt!"

Mama answered, "No, it doesn't matter. I never wanted her anyway."

"How can you say that? She's your child!"

Everything went black. I broke out of the cocoon. In seconds, I soared through the clouds, leaving the painful, ugly scene below. Though my guardian angel was with me, he was too slow. I zoomed ahead of him and saw the corner of a glass building. The colors were so beautiful. Peach, mauve, and a pale sky-blue sparkled on the building, the reflection of the sunset on the glass.

Abruptly, we stopped, turned, and I looked through the clouds at the scene below. I knew I had to go back. We plummeted downward, back toward the country store.

When we got closer to the scene, I saw Mama facing the lady, who stood by the store wall surrounded by three children. While the lady looked over Mama's shoulder at the dead little girl, two of the children, who appeared to be twins, hid their faces in her skirt. The other child stood frozen against the store wall. Mama, jostling Lori, ignored the scene behind her.

Daddy crouched down by the dead little girl's head. He gently moved the hair away from her left ear, talking to her. I knew she was me. I swooped in close to the little girl's head and looked up at Daddy. Tears poured down his face and dripped from his chin. I couldn't hear what he said, but there is no question what he felt. The love on his face, so deeply painful at that moment, moved me. I didn't want Daddy to hurt. Everything went black again.

Jesus reminded me, *"He pleaded for your life."*

The next time my eyelids parted, I saw something pink through the fog, pink gauze.

Someone held a pink gauze dress to my face. While I struggled to open my eyes more, she moved the dress, and I could see a hospital bed with rails on both sides. Though I couldn't move my head, I saw some of the room.

Two strangers stood by the bedrail on the right, talking low. The lady stranger had her hand on the dress she'd placed down by my feet on the white blanket covering me. Both of them were dressed well. The lady wore a short-sleeved white dress with lots of tiny dark dots on it. Her white cardigan sweater hung limply from her shoulders. I liked her hat, sitting tilted on her head. It was small, round, and white with white netting and tiny flowers on it. The man wore a gray suit and held his hat in his hands. They both looked very sad.

Tubes and metal machines were everywhere. In a sweet voice, Mama told me that as soon as I got well, I would be able to wear that pretty dress. She leaned up and put her hand on my foot. I felt her hand but then realized I couldn't move any part of me. I couldn't talk because something filled my mouth, but I didn't care. I had nothing to say. I was tired, and I didn't want to be there. I didn't want to be anywhere.

The strangers said something softly to Daddy and left. Mama sat back down on the stool beside a machine at the end of my bed. She moved the machine over and said it was too crowded in there. Daddy shushed her. Not sweet anymore, through gritted teeth, she whispered something to Daddy, who sat to my left. Out of the corner of my eye, I saw his right hand on the bed rail, and his legs were crossed so I could see his navy-issued black shoes and blue jeans. I was so glad he was there. He shushed Mama again. She didn't like it. Her face looked so mean. How could she be so sweet one minute and so mean the next? Daddy held my hand, and I drifted off to sleep.

I told Paul I first needed to deal with Mama's threatening to throw Lori out of the window. My anger boiled. How could she do such a thing? How could a mother even think of throwing her child out of the window of a moving car?

Paul asked me if Jesus could take the anger away. I thought, *Why keep it?* I agreed, and Jesus did. Under my anger lay fear. The thought of Lori flying through the air and landing who knew where terrified me. As a child, I didn't think of her dying on impact, I just thought she'd be lying there in the grass, alone. She would cry, and no one would be there to hold her. After Jesus removed the fear, unforgiveness remained. (I'd done this so many times. I felt I could go through the process in my sleep.)

Choosing to forgive and get rid of the debt, I gave Jesus the hand-sized rock. He laid it at the foot of the cross. Lori, who was not so helpless and fragile anymore, didn't need me to guard her.

Next, I knew I had to face the last large rock in the box. Mama didn't want me. All my life I'd tried to please her and earn her love. Paul asked me what she owed me.

I whispered, "Love. I just wanted her to love me."

Jesus spoke up softly, *"She didn't know how."*

Instead of love, she filled up the space reserved for her in my heart with pain and suffering. That piece of my heart eventually turned to stone.

I gave Jesus the only remaining large rock from the box. It was the one that filled Mama's place in my heart. I felt so hollow, watching Him place it at the cross. As He stepped back over to me, the emptiness grew. In the center of my being, there was a vast, gaping hole. I had starved for love, for the knowledge that I mattered to someone. My body became a paper-thin shell of emptiness, almost completely invisible.

I was weak and barely able to stand; Jesus steadied me. He then turned and stepped aside, giving place to the only One who could give me what I needed. Love, Himself, moved into place in front of me. From a cloud-like form with sparkling lights at its center, His hand reached out toward me. The moment His pointing finger connected with the void at my center, absolute and indescribable love began pouring into me. The warmth calmed and strengthened me, giving me substance. While Jesus looked on, love completely filled the hole in me.

I described the scene to Paul, who sat amazed. I told him the only thing I could think of that came close to describing that feeling was getting up in the morning, starving, as if I hadn't eaten in a month, and eating a bowl of perfectly cooked, perfectly flavored oatmeal. The warm smoothness settled my stomach, and the sweet satisfaction filled my hollow core.

Paul asked, "Jesus, is there anything You'd like Carly to know about this?"

Jesus told me God couldn't pour His love into me like that until I gave up the unforgiveness and debt. He then took every negative feeling I'd listed to Paul earlier in the session—worthlessness, unloved, stupid, can't do anything right—exposed the lies, and revealed the truth about each one. I listened closely, letting each word sink in.

"*Worthless? Had you been the only one, I would have died for you. You are worth My blood. Unloved? God Himself loves you with an unending, unlimited love. Stupid? Hardly. You have accomplishments. Can't do anything right? That is a matter of opinion. Correctness isn't always best determined by the other person. Some people get in a sour mood, and nothing you do for them seems right. That doesn't mean it isn't. Use good sense.*"

He went on to say He would always be there for me, and when my time on Earth was complete, I could live with Him forever. Nothing would ever stop Him from loving me—complete, unconditional love.

Mama didn't love me, never had. That's all right. God does and always has. My pastor once said we don't come from our parents; we come from God through our parents. God knew about me when I was in my mother's womb. He loved me then and continues to love me. His love never stops; it never fails. On the day I return to Him, the enormity of His love is what will make heaven heavenly to me.

It is the parents' responsibility to love and care for the child on loan to them. Even when they don't, God does. He will step in as needed and either make the child strong or take the child home. He made me strong. I belong to God, and belonging matters. He knows my name. He is the center of my universe.

I am come that they might have life, and that they might have it more abundantly.
—John 10:10b

18

Macie's graduation from college put all of us in the spirit of celebration. We drove several hours to spend a few days with her and attend the ceremony. While her husband proudly videoed the event, Grant stood near, a look of satisfaction on his face. I held my breath, as pleased as any mother could be, watching Macie walk across the stage clutching that well-earned piece of paper.

I had been in her shoes many years prior and knew that on that day, she really didn't know the full impact of what she'd accomplished. On the first day of her new job, when she realized she could make a positive impact on the lives of others, and then the day she held that first week's paycheck, knowing she could do what she loved and someone would actually pay her for it, then she'd understand that every sacrifice had been worth it.

Macie's two teenage boys stood at attention beside Anna. They were proud and happy, but not one of the three was comfortable in their dressy apparel; they were ready to go. *One day*, I thought, *perhaps we will have the privilege of standing proudly as one of them walks across a stage to receive a college diploma.* When asked why I was smiling, I replied, "I'm just proud."

While we were in town, my girls and I went by to visit Mama. The girls didn't know the details of my memories. They only knew I visited a counselor for some childhood problems. April, my youngest sister, told Mama, several weeks before the visit, all she knew about my therapy. That was fine; I hadn't told her much. Maybe one day Mama and I could talk about it, but I had already decided it would not be on this visit.

Mama appeared at her door, exhausted. She had been diagnosed with a blood disorder akin to leukemia, and her doctor put her through a gamut of tests and different treatments, attempting to find the right one to cure her. Mama liked her doctor and felt he would eventually figure out the problem. As she talked, slowly and frequently stopping for a breath, I felt like I did when visiting an elderly lady I hardly knew from our church. At that moment, I realized I had no feelings for her. None. Nor for anyone else. I looked at my daughters and felt nothing. That scared me.

Mama redirected my thoughts by saying she had a picture set aside to give me. "It's my favorite one of you," she added. When Macie retrieved it from the bookshelf and handed it to me, I saw she had framed my first-grade school picture. Mama asked me if I remembered the green dress I wore for the picture. I did. She knew it was my favorite dress. I called it my Girl Scout dress.

I never participated in Girl Scouts, but the dress looked very similar to the ones they wore. I wore it to school on the same day the real Girl Scouts wore theirs. I felt like I fit in with them. What struck me most about the picture, though, was the way the dress was buttoned. I had looked at that picture a million times and never noticed it before. Every button fastened, right up to my throat.

My mind swirled. Is that the way the real Girl Scouts wore theirs? They had a little tie I didn't have. I thought of all the pictures I had of me as a child. Up to age four, I wore sunsuits and other outfits with my upper chest showing. After that, most of the pictures had that part of me covered. I have scars, but I'd always thought they were normal rowdy-child kind of scars. I'd have to explore that line of thinking more but at another time.

We stayed at Mama's less than half an hour. Jake, my youngest brother, had done excellent work on her apartment. It fit her life perfectly. I told her I wished she didn't feel tired all the time and hoped she'd be better soon. Words. Just words. I didn't feel a thing.

When I shared all of this with Lori later, she suggested Mama could have given me the picture to open up the conversation and apologize. Maybe she didn't say it because my girls were there.

The girls later told me that while I was in the bathroom at Mama's house, Mama sat in her living room chair, whispering through gritted teeth, " Liar, liar, liar." Over and over she said it. Macie said it was creepy.

After prayer, I decided I needed to stay away from her—for her sake as well as mine. I think just being around me awakens something bad in her, which could have been why she struggled so hard to breathe that day. Anxiety can do that.

Wendy called after we returned home from Macie's. I told her about our trip and visit with Mama. She and April believed my problems stemmed from things Daddy had done. They didn't know the details of my counseling sessions, so they insisted Mama loved me. I repeatedly said to them, "She told me as a child that she hated me. And Mama, not Daddy, abused me." Actions speak louder than words. They were loved by Mama and still thought I was in denial. Mama's constant berating of Daddy was firmly planted in their minds. Daddy was far from perfect; I know that. He was an alcoholic, and he didn't always make the best decisions. Even drunk, though, I never saw him do anything with malice.

I remember a time when Daddy took Dean and me into a world we didn't even know existed. When Dean turned six, he had to get a physical before starting school. A spot showed up on the lung x-ray, and the doctor said it could be the beginning of tuberculosis. The school system wouldn't allow him to enter first grade, so he stayed home and started school with me the next year. The spot disappeared before the following fall. School were segregated until the early sixties, so even if we had started school, we wouldn't have known there were kids out there whose skin wasn't as pale as ours.

That hot summer afternoon, we overheard Daddy tell Mama he was going to the store. I begged him to take Dean and me with him. He nodded but added we'd have to stay in the car. We agreed. (Would that make this whole episode our fault?)

Ecstatic, we piled into the backseat of the car and laughed and giggled all the way there. Daddy pulled up under the front shelter of an old run-down wooden building and turned the car off. He got out, telling us we were in the shade so we shouldn't get too hot, and he'd be back in a little while. We nodded. The hot, dusty air poured in through the rolled-down windows, but we were happy to be out and about, away from the house and Mama.

After a short while, we heard some kids talking. They came up to the car and looked in at us. Dean and I had never seen anyone like them. They had never seen anyone like us either. My bright red hair fascinated one kid so much she reached in and tried to grab some of it. I think she just wanted to feel it because the texture of my hair was very different from hers. She appeared to be older than we were. The insides of her hands were lighter than the rest of her dusty, dark skin, and her teeth were incredibly white and big. The rest of them followed her lead and also stretched their arms into the car as far as they could. I was scared spitless.

Dean and I held each other in the middle of the seat, just out of contact of the hands reaching in on both sides of us. Dean told me to close my eyes. He always said that when he knew I was scared. (Once he led me all the way through a Halloween spook house with my eyes closed. Otherwise, he knew I'd have choked him by climbing on his back with my arms around his neck.)

Soon, the dark kids tired of us and went inside the store. As soon as they did, we rolled up the windows. A few minutes later another group of kids came with the same skin color, the same incredibly white teeth, and the same braided hair sticking up all over their heads. This time they pressed their faces against the glass, trying to see us. Flattened noses, bulging eyes, and big white teeth ... I closed my eyes again until Dean said they were gone.

We thought about going in to get Daddy, but neither one of us was willing to leave the car. So we waited. There were so many black kids coming and going we figured we must have been near where they lived. Some of them came out drinking a dark drink in a bottle. I was thirsty, but I didn't want any of that. My five-year-old mind decided that was why their skin was so dark. No "pale skins" went into that store except Daddy. We didn't know what planet we were on.

After the sun went down, the air cooled. Soon, Daddy came out. He had been drinking and acted goofy, but we were sure glad to see him. We asked him about the strange-looking kids, and while he drove home, he explained about black people being different yet the same. He laughed when I told him they tried to grab my hair. I didn't think it was funny. He went on to explain that their skin and hair on the outside look different from ours, but on the inside we're all the same. I didn't know whether to believe that or not. I'd have to think about that for a while. I certainly didn't want to grab their hair. The whole situation scared me so bad I didn't ask to go with Daddy to the store for a long time afterward. Years later, I came to the conclusion that Daddy was pretty smart, even when he was drunk, and that RC Cola does not darken one's skin.

Another not-so-great decision Daddy made occurred around the time of April's birth. We all went with Daddy when he took Mama to the hospital. It was summer, too hot to stay in the car on the scorching asphalt of the hospital's treeless parking lot, so Daddy had to figure out what to do with us. Babysitters were hard to come by for four kids, particularly a seven-year-old like me. I didn't like any of them, and after one time, they usually declined to come back. Daddy decided he'd babysit us and take us to the lake for a picnic. We made some sandwiches, packed some drinks and potato chips, and headed out.

After lunch, I begged Daddy to let us ride down the shoreline on the car hood. The top of each of the car's headlights curved so a kid could straddle it like a rocking horse. We had done this before when Mama picnicked with us. Only Dean and I rode, though, holding on to the car. Mama didn't care as long as Daddy drove slowly.

That day, he had had a few beers with his sandwich and agreed to take us for a ride. He wanted us to have fun. Dean and I decided the other two would have fun riding too. We didn't think about having only two hands to hold on to them and the car at the same time. I sat three-year-old Lori in front of me on the left headlight, and Dean held on to Wendy, who was two, while straddling the right. Daddy crept along. Disappointed because our hair didn't even blow, we begged him to go faster. He sped up some. Wendy wiggled, and Dean dropped her. Daddy stopped the car, but we had to dig Wendy out of the soft sand beneath the front part of the right front tire. We all got back in the car. Wendy wouldn't stop crying; her diaper turned red. I told Daddy, who sobered up quick and rushed back to the hospital.

Wendy spent three weeks in traction with a fractured pelvis. Daddy spent overnight in jail. Dana and Keith, our next-door neighbors, came over to stay the night with us just before the police picked Daddy up.

He made us go out on the back porch before the police came. He didn't want us to see them take him away. He was sad.

When he came home the next day, he told us he had gone by to visit Mama with the new baby, and Wendy. They were all doing just fine. I asked him if Mama could visit Wendy too. He said, "Yeah, she can."

Later, I found out Mama didn't know about Wendy's accident until the day she came home with April. Daddy dreaded telling her. I didn't blame him. I felt I was to blame for the accident. I had begged him to let us ride, but I sure didn't tell Mama. In situations like that, the less said, the better off we all were.

Like all of us, Wendy at times could get herself into trouble—but she was a toddler. We were older and supposed to be watching (protecting, guiding) her. Isn't that what family members do for each other?

Wendy was about a year old when she had a run-in with the coffee percolator. I was six. She was just learning to walk and pulled up on anything, including people, if they would let her. She loved to stand up. It made her giddy. The look of triumph on her face when she pulled up and stood there made me giggle. We enjoyed helping her learn to walk because she got so excited about it. Sometimes I laughed so hard at her excitement I couldn't even walk forward with her, so she'd stand, leaning forward, wobbling her fat little legs, at which I laughed even harder.

Everything around her fascinated her. One could tell by the look in her eyes she wanted to know more about whatever was in view. I guess that is why she got so excited about walking; she wanted to get into everything.

On that particular afternoon, Mama and Daddy were dancing with some friends in the living room. As they did the Stroll to Fats Domino's "Walking to New Orleans," Dean and I kept the two younger kids occupied in the kitchen/dining room area. The music was loud, and we loved it. The grown-ups had already put the coffee on, and we were to tell them when it was ready.

Wendy pulled up and stood by a chair near the kitchen counter, where the percolator was plugged into the wall. Her stubby fingers wrapped around the cord, jerked it a few times, and pulled it to her mouth for a taste. Before I could get to her, the percolator tipped off of the counter and crashed onto the tile floor. Its lid popped off when it hit, and boiling coffee flooded the floor.

Lori, just two years old, sat on the floor nearby, playing. As boiling coffee spilled over Wendy's lower body and began to reach Lori, they both screamed, bringing Mama and Daddy running. The coffee had soaked Lori's underwear as she struggled to get her feet under her. Carefully placing my feet, I jerked Wendy up, but the coffee had already done its damage.

Mama and Daddy grabbed Wendy, iced her down, and rushed to the emergency room. Parts of Wendy's lower body were so cooked that the skin slid around on them, and she suffered major scarring that was evident for years.

The friends stayed with the rest of us at the house. In the confusion, Lori was ignored. The friends cleaned up the coffee and, in the process, realized Lori too had been scalded. They changed her clothes and treated her burns. She suffered blistering burns on her bottom but no physical scarring. She certainly couldn't sit for a while. The real scarring came from being ignored while she screamed in pain, left to suffer on her own. That day, one more was added to the long string of invisible moments for Lori and the long string of unhappy events for Wendy.

Wendy had not only learned to walk but to run and climb. On another unfortunate occasion, I was in charge of watching her while Daddy worked on the hot water heater, and Mama put clothes in the washer. She measured bleach into a coffee cup and set it on the countertop, waiting for the washer to fill and begin agitation so she could add the bleach.

While Mama busied herself in the bedrooms, Wendy busied herself in the kitchen. She climbed up onto a bar stool, about to help herself to what she thought was Mama's or Daddy's cold cup of coffee. When she saw me coming to get her down, she grabbed the cup quickly and drank some, determined to have a sip, her eyes on me instead of the drink in the cup. The sour look on her face would've made me laugh, if it hadn't scared me so bad.

I screamed for Mama. "Wendy drank the bleach!" Mama came running and washed her mouth out repeatedly while Wendy screamed. Luckily, she only sipped a small amount. A trip to the emergency room confirmed that only her mouth and back of her throat were affected. From then on, Dean and I had to stay within an arm's length of a younger sibling when we were in charge.

After April's birth, she became Daddy's favorite. In fact, Mama let him name her. As the tiniest one of us all, she stole our hearts. While Wendy was a chubby baby, cute and cuddly, April's tiny frame was wiry, and she looked like a doll. She may have been more difficult to cuddle, but loving her took no effort. That big-girl attitude in such a little body delighted everyone.

When she learned to talk, *no* was a word she used often to show disapproval. She was so cute, frowning, pointing her tiny finger, and saying, "No!" We all laughed. She then realized she could make us laugh, so she turned it into a production. She yelled, "No, no, no," with one finger pointing while the other fingers on that hand were sticking out in all directions. Her legs bounced and then her knees locked with every "no!" She watched our faces and expected us to laugh. We knew she was trying to entertain us, and of course we laughed. We also knew she'd never allow anyone to run over her, little or not.

We loved every child who came along. When Jake made his appearance, there were six of us. Mama had a difficult time bouncing back after his birth. She slept or cried all of the time. Daddy needed some adult help, so he enlisted our neighbors, Keith and Dana. They were good friends, and Daddy let them take care of Jake at their house until Mama could get back on her feet.

Keith and Dana had no children of their own and had already won our hearts by letting us play in their backyard. Keith even played tag with us in the evening when he was home from work. He loved children, just like our daddy did. They were both wonderful people, and I knew Jake would be fine. He was right next door, and we could go over to see him anytime we wanted. Mama thought Daddy was giving Jake away and that she'd never see him again. It made her cry even more, so Keith and Dana brought him back. Mama called Grandma, and she came to help.

Daddy and Grandma usually got along pretty good. He even took her fishing a number of times when she came to stay with us. Dean and I were old enough that sometimes they let us go with them. Grandma loved to fish with a cane pole from the bank. Daddy placed all of her fishing stuff around her chair and told us to help her if she needed anything. He usually went to the end of the dock or out in a borrowed boat to fish. Grandma couldn't swim, so she declined when he invited her into the boat. She said the bank was the best place for her.

Daddy did his best to accommodate her, and things went pretty well. Grandma had her opinions, though, as well as a backhanded slap that could wake the dead. Daddy quickly let her know she wouldn't be slapping him. She didn't slap us either when he was around.

In fact, Daddy's presence made everything different. We laughed more and were allowed to be kids. He sent us out to play while he and Mama (and Grandma, if she was there) did the housework and cooking. He kept Mama away from us and us away from her. Mama had his attention most of the time. It was what she wanted, and so that was okay. Just his being there made me happy.

Mama never pulled out the cord when he was there. She'd threaten, but the cord only came out when Daddy was gone. In his absence, she turned into a different person, full of anger or deep depression. During counseling, when I remembered Mama's face from long ago, cold chills washed over me.

When Daddy scolded us, it was out of normal parental frustration. I have no recollection of his ever spanking me. When he scolded, the disappointed look on his face was punishment enough for me. I wanted to please him. He never wanted any of us to experience pain, especially when we were small. His face filled with love and concern when we did get hurt. I still see his face, tears dripping from his chin, pleading for my life.

When any of his children suffered, he didn't take it lightly. But any time he tried to show us love, Mama showed her disapproval. She could not keep him from loving us, so she determined to stop us from loving him—especially April, his favorite. Mama berated him every chance she got and made every effort to turn us against him. As we grew older, he tired of the battle and just tried to provide for us. He stopped feeling anything and became a shell. He seemed happiest when he was in his garden, alone.

Several days after I talked to Wendy about my visit with Mama, I called Paul and told him I couldn't feel anything. It had been about ten days, and I worried it might be permanent. Paul said there was a reason for it and that I should not to try to wake up my feelings until I sat in his office. I didn't know how to wake them up anyway. Apparently, Daddy didn't either.

19

In Paul's office that Thursday, we prayed and began. Jesus reminded me of my pastor's statement: "We come from God, through our parents. I belong to God."

A memory opened up.

> I was six. Mama was wearing a red sleeveless shirt and black Capri pants, called pedal-pushers, with thin red and white stripes down the side seam. She brushed past me and began ironing in front of the TV. Dean and Lori sat on the couch, while I sat on the floor, watching *Superman* through the clothes.
>
> I heard a sizzle and watched Mama hurry into the kitchen, making a crying noise. I was afraid she was badly hurt and followed her, asking "Are you okay? Can I see? Mama? Why are you crying? Are you okay? Mama?" She didn't answer, so I kept on asking.
>
> She leaned on the counter in the kitchen, holding an ice tray wrapped in a wet towel to her arm. When I continued to question, she turned to me and screamed, "Shut up, shut up, shut up! Don't you ever *shut up*?"
>
> I backed up like I'd been slapped. Seeing my hurt, her eyes narrowed and cut into me as she spoke. "I hate you! You hear me? Get out of my sight. I don't even want to look at you!"

I felt so alone. I had no one. I found my way back to the living room, a rock in my throat. My chest felt heavy; my arms and legs were too tired to move another inch. I looked at the TV and made myself focus on it. I stared at it, but all I thought about was how much she hated me. It hurt too much. The TV blurred. I turned off the pain. Numb was better.

Paul talked to me about forgiveness.

"Yes, I want to forgive her," I said. "I want to get rid of the rocks in my box."

I gave Jesus two hand-sized rocks from my box, one for her screaming at me, the other for her rejecting my affection. He then talked to me about my love for Mama. *What? How could I love her when she treated me so bad?*

Jesus said He was there every time she mistreated me. My feelings awakened as I remembered. Tears fell.

I remembered his voice talking to me, encouraging me, and showing me how to love her, even when she hurt me. There were times when the voice came out of nowhere and led me to a safe place in the house. At times, I ended up in the back corner of my bunk bed, with my blanket wadded in front of me, or flat on my belly under the metal-framed couch, or behind the curtains where no one could see me. I stood perfectly still, like a statue. Invisible—that was my desire, to fade into nothing. There, in my invisible state, the voice explained that Mama didn't want to be mean; sometimes she just couldn't help it. He told me to love the good part of her and stay away when the bad part came to life. I followed His instruction, hoping that one day Bad Mama would never show up again. I remembered, too, when I felt confused and hurt, the voice told me it wasn't my fault, explaining each situation in language I understood, carefully molding and shaping me with His words. He is the reason I'm not a resident at a mental health facility.

In reality, knowing all I know now, I don't want to love Mama. It hurts to love someone who doesn't love me, especially when that someone is my mother. Yet there was a compassion that settled in my heart when I let go of the negative stranglehold the hurt had on me. I couldn't help it. I gave Jesus the unforgiveness, the anger, and the hate. God filled me with His love, His compassion, and His grace for the hurting.

I don't love her like a child loves a mother. Jesus didn't ask me to do that. He asked me to love her as God does. It's not about a mother/daughter relationship. I don't think that will ever be a reality between us. I believe I understand God's love better now and can honestly say I love the broken little girl who lives in that seventy-something-year-old body, so desperately needing a Father to love her. I hope and pray she'll let Him.

20

Snap, crackle, and pop are the sounds I get up to every morning. The older I get, the louder and more painful my body becomes. I have always been somewhat off center, but my body compensated. Now, I'm less flexible, and the pain in my shoulder, lower back, and hip has increased in intensity. While I do have a high tolerance for pain, there is a limit.

I went to the doctor, and he ordered x-rays after he saw the unevenness of my rib cage and sagging right side. With the x-ray, he could pinpoint the problem and determine treatment. I told him I had been in a car accident as a young child and wondered if it had affected my skeleton. I had never heard Mama or Daddy discuss the accident or broken bones.

As an adult, my arms are different lengths, as are my legs, but it's almost unnoticeable. When I put them together, I adjust my body until they match. I thought everybody did that. I'd seen others in much worse shape than I was.

When I was in the second grade, a boy at my school had a severely abnormal spine. It curved in an S-shape, and he had difficulty with even the most minor of motor skills. I was a bit afraid of him; anything unusual in people scared me. He couldn't play games with the rest of us, so he sat with the teacher. Sometimes, though I was nervous, I went over and talked to him. I felt sorry for him and was thankful my back stood straight. At that time, it did.

A complete set of thoracic and lumbar x-rays revealed the cause of my pain: several old fractures. Two fractures in the pelvic and right hip area. My right leg is almost an inch and a half shorter than my left, causing my pelvis to tilt dramatically and causing the pain in my lower back and hip. The doctor explained that I finished growing between the ages of eighteen and twenty-five. The right leg grew at a slower rate because of the damaged growth plate.

In my upper skeleton, my left clavicle had been broken and displaced. The bone was not set, so it grew back overlapped, making the left clavicle quite a bit shorter than the right one. My rib cage was damaged and skewed, causing one side to be lower than the other by an inch or two. One top left rib is bowed outward, and my spine is noticeably bent, compensating for the short clavicle.

Several ribs showed old fracture marks, and the doctor said I probably suffered a collapsed lung when it happened. I thought about the machines in my room and the tubes in my throat at the hospital but didn't mention them.

He said, "It's a wonder you lived through it."

There was much I wanted to say, but the mind-set of "Don't sound like a mental patient" kicked in, and I just said, "Uh-huh."

He determined little could be done to straighten my upper back permanently because of the short clavicle and scapula that grew to match it. Adjustments now and then would help ease the upper spinal and shoulder pain.

An orthopedic heel lift placed in my right shoe somewhat corrected my hip alignment and alleviated quite a bit of the pain there. I walked up and down the hall at the doctor's office, amazed at the difference. With continued adjustments, my skeletal structure and corresponding muscles are lining up, and the pain level has diminished.

As with most people, when I hurt, walking around or adjusting the way I sit helps to alleviate the pain. Knowing the truth about the accident does too. A few years before my counseling and these x-rays revealed my true skeletal history, I broke my foot playing volleyball barefooted in the gym with my coworkers. I told Mama it was the first time I had ever broken a bone. She agreed.

21

I woke up at 3:25 a.m. Wide awake. A memory flashed through my mind.

> Daddy's face. I stared up at him. He smiled at someone to my left. I stood at his knee, my stubby fingers gripping his blue jeans. His left hand covered and secured my fingers to make sure I didn't fall. Sunlight poured into the kitchen, and Daddy smelled like coffee.

He looked like pictures of him at about the age of twenty-eight. That would make my age around two. He was so handsome. I loved his smile and that coffee smell. Comforted, I drifted back to sleep.

At 5:20, awakened by the alarm, I saw Daddy's face again. I lay there and let the memory unfold.

> His smile turned into a grin when he looked down at me. "Come on." He pulled me up by one arm. I grabbed his white T-shirt and scrambled onto his lap. He had a present for me. I was so excited.
>
> From behind his back he brought out a white bangle bracelet. I held it in my hands, turning it this way and that. It was beautiful. The white hard-plastic bracelet, sized just right for me, was decorated with four clusters of roses spaced evenly apart. Daddy

said, "Put it on your arm. Slide it up like this." I watched him make the motion with his own arm and a pretend bracelet.

Before I could put it on my arm, Mama snatched it out of my hand. I cried. She yelled at Daddy while she held the bracelet inches from his nose. They argued. He left and I crawled under the kitchen table to hide. She was scary when she was angry.

I never saw that bracelet again. As I prepared Grant's lunch cooler for work, I wondered what happened to the bracelet. And I wondered if Mama hated me because Daddy brought me presents.

Some years before Paul Thompson Counseling, I had asked Mama why she mistreated me more than her other children. My being treated far worse than my siblings was common knowledge among us, but the details were never discussed. To me, the abuse was just a fact of life, the monster in my closet. I kept the door tightly locked, sure it would stay there. I didn't see the need to know the details; I just wanted to know why I was singled out.

Mama answered that because I looked like Daddy's mama, auburn hair and all, she couldn't stand me. She went on about what a terrible person Daddy's mama was and how she died a horrible death. I thought maybe that is why Daddy paid particular attention to me. His mama died before I was born.

Evidence was building to support the theory that Mama wanted Daddy to love only her and no one else. She didn't love Daddy; she just wanted to be the center of his affection. If Daddy gave any love to anyone else, it seemed that Mama set out to destroy that person in Daddy's eyes or to destroy Daddy in that person's eyes. Either way, she would break that bond.

A few days after the bracelet memory opened up, I called Lori and told her about it. She said she remembered Mama telling her about

Daddy bringing me presents without something for Dean. She said she took them because it wasn't fair.

Mama told Lori of a time when Daddy came home with a candy bar in his sock. When he gave it to me, Mama took it, cut it into two pieces and handed them to Dean and me. It wasn't the sharing that bothered me, but that Mama always took anything Daddy gave me. He soon stopped bringing home presents.

Is that why I never expected anything good to happen to me? If something good did come my way, I knew it wouldn't last. I came to realize that I could be stripped of anything I had at any time. This was a problem for Paul's office.

A few days before my next appointment, another memory opened.

> I knelt on the floor by the kitchen table, the silver rim at eye level. Near me, Mama sat leaning over a pan, peeling potatoes. Daddy, over by the sink, talked very fast, moving his hands around. He laughed and stretched his hands wide like he was talking about a big fish someone caught. While he talked, her face reddened. He couldn't see her face. I could. He talked on.
>
> She clenched her teeth. Uh-oh! Silver eyes, sharp knife. The blade flashed in the light. She lunged for him. He scrambled and got away. My heart screamed, *Run, Daddy, run!* I pulled Lori, who was still learning to walk, under the table with me. We hid for a while. Daddy was gone again.

I didn't know whether to deal with the bracelet memory or the sharp knife memory first, so I told Paul we'd just let Jesus decide. When we prayed, the bracelet memory opened. It progressed just as I had seen it. Then a string of similar memories streamed through my mind. All had the same meaning: Daddy loved me. His gifts were sometimes just a hug, a kiss, or a moment of being comforted in his lap. Other times, he brought me some little trinket or snack. Mama always got mad and threw a fit. Then he'd leave.

At the end of the string of memories, Daddy lay dead on the bathroom floor, his feet in the hallway. That time he wouldn't come back late in the night, slip in, and touch our cheeks with a kiss. That time, she made him leave forever. That time, she took everything.

In Paul's office, I cried. I missed Daddy every time he left. I said, "I miss him terribly now. He'd be eighty years old, and I know I'm too big to sit in his lap, but I'd love to hug him and talk to him. I'd beg him to live with us. He'd like my cooking. Why did this happen? How could she do this to him and to us?"

Paul asked, "Do you sense any unforgiveness?"

"No ... no unforgiveness, anger, or hate. Just a deep sadness."

"Will you let Jesus take the sadness away and see what happens?"

"No, it's all I have left of Daddy. If the sadness goes away, I'm afraid I will lose him completely."

"Jesus, what do you want Carly to know about that?"

Jesus said, *"Let the sadness go. Trust me; you'll see. It's better to let it go."*

Unsure but trusting Him, I said, "Okay, Jesus, please take the sadness away."

The sadness left. I felt nothing. My emotions suspended in thin air; the void captured my attention.

Jesus said, *"He's here with me."*

As if awakened and unsure of what I'd heard, I blurted out, "What? What did you say?"

I sat up straighter on Paul's sofa, alert, focusing only on my inner self with my hands still over my closed eyes.

Paul broke in. "What's going on?"

"Wait a minute. I need to hear something."

Jesus, what did you say again? Please tell me one more time. I'm listening!

A scene opened. A light fog rolled in the air. As the fog cleared, someone stood there, his back to me. He had dark hair and wore a white, long-sleeved collared shirt. I saw the sleeves rolled up a certain way.

"Is it?" He turned around and looked at me, taking my breath away. "Daddy! It is you!"

His face beamed; a beautiful smile stretched ear to ear. I'd never seen him happier.

"He's with me," Jesus repeated, *"in heaven."*

I wept for joy as I told Paul. I had often wondered if Daddy even had the chance to pray. He never talked about God or his beliefs. He wasn't much of a talker about anything later in life. When I gave Jesus the sadness, He gave me joy.

Oh, wow! Daddy waits for us in heaven! When we get there, Mama can never make him leave us again. I was so excited.

I called Lori on my cell phone as I sped down the parkway toward home. She cheered, excited to know Daddy is in heaven. I couldn't wait to get home and write in my journal. Eternity became brighter and sweeter that day.

Iridescent Grace

I woke up the next morning, and the battle began. My recently recalled memories of Daddy fought the picture of him Mama had painted for us through the years. The memories of Daddy—a man with a good heart, loving his children, trying to be a father to them—have been revived and are stronger now than ever. They are old and were buried deep, but the love is real.

As my siblings and I grew up, Mama's ugly words were powerful and persistent. Daddy grew tired of fighting her to love us, so he shrunk back, letting her words take center stage. In truth, Daddy never stood a chance.

Daddy experienced his share of pain as a child. His parents split up when he was young. His mother, Belle, moved a hundred miles away without her daughter and four sons and remarried. The children remained in their hometown with Perry, their dad. Times were hard in the 1940s, and work was difficult to find. Perry worked out of town quite a bit and finally remarried. That woman's brother, it is told, was responsible for Perry's death—something about a life insurance policy. It didn't work out for him, though. Perry had changed the beneficiary to his mom.

They had no one after Perry was killed, so they were forced to care for themselves. Extended family members were struggling to feed their own families. Who could take in five more hungry mouths? Daddy and his older sister, Carla, quit school to care for the three younger siblings. Carla cooked and cleaned for them. Daddy, then about twelve, used his skill with a rifle to help feed the family. Rabbits, squirrels, and other small game were plentiful in the backwoods.

Daddy's uncle told me he saw Daddy long ago use a tin can lid to reflect the bright sunlight into a bird's eyes to blind it so he could catch it. He said Daddy did that over and over until he had enough for supper. Life was tough.

Daddy reconnected with his mother in southern Georgia when he was about fourteen. He enrolled at the junior high school there and worked at a mayonnaise plant to help make ends meet. Then, a week after his eighteenth birthday, Daddy joined the US Navy. Many years later, following a failed marriage and while visiting his mother, he met and fell in love with Mama.

Sometime after Mama and Daddy married, Belle was hospitalized with appendicitis. During the surgery, her intestines were accidentally stitched closed. By the time the mistake surfaced, gangrene had already set in. Even though Belle had deserted Daddy at the worst possible time, Daddy stood by her side as she passed away. He loved her. That is why Mama hated her. I've been told Belle didn't like Mama either from the moment they met.

Mama had her own share of baggage. She hated many people but none more than her own daddy. His cruelty earned her hate. But why did she want us to hate our daddy? The only answer was his love for us.

He wasn't cruel. The only times I saw him angry were when Mama antagonized and manipulated him. She threw boiling-hot coffee on him, scratched him or slapped him, and complained about anything and everything. Nothing ever suited her. When they fought, he'd leave, and she'd fill our heads with ugliness about him. Then he'd come home drunk, and she'd bellow at him about that. She went on and on about how our lives would be better if he weren't around. Eventually, we began to believe her, and he gave up. He said to her one time, "All I've ever wanted is for you to love me."

She answered, "I don't love you. I never will."

He retreated into his shell, no emotion left.

My youngest siblings grew to hate him. They never got to know the real Daddy. I never hated him; he just seemed distant.

During the therapy sessions, I felt Daddy's love again, just as I had in my early childhood. I have always loved him; I just didn't realize it. And I had forgotten how it felt to be loved by a father, a caregiver, someone bigger and stronger than I am, to whom I belong.

At Lori's suggestion, I began to carry pictures of Daddy that closely matched my memories of him. Every time Mama's face appeared, saying bad things about Daddy, I'd take out the picture and study his face, letting myself remember the love that came through his eyes. And I cried. It was a truth-knowing, lie-disintegrating, healing-of-a-little-girl's-heart kind of cry.

After finding out all of these things about Daddy in his records and the memories I have of him, my heart broke that he'd died alone, with no apparent love from anyone. I talked to Paul about it after we had opened with prayer in one of our sessions. He said we should go back into the memory of Daddy's death and see what Jesus said. I wasn't sure I wanted to feel the pain of that night again, but I was willing to try.

The memory opened up easily, and I saw Daddy's feet in the hallway.

Paul told me to ask Jesus where He was during this time. "He was there," Paul said.

"No, He wasn't!" I blurted out. "How could He have been? There was so much evil there. How could He have been in all that?" I did not understand.

Paul said to stay in the memory and find Him. So I did.

> I stepped into the hallway and over to Daddy's feet. He was still gurgling and trying to talk. I couldn't understand anything he was saying. When I looked into the bathroom where he lay dying, I saw Jesus kneeling at Daddy's head. He told him to relax and let go.
>
> Daddy said, "I'm scared."

Jesus said, "I know."

"I'm scared of leaving them with her."

"It's okay. They will be fine. I will take care of them." Jesus waited.

Daddy relaxed and let go. He and Jesus moved up and away from me. Daddy's body lay quiet and still.

I told Paul everything as it happened. Tears fell when I told him Daddy relaxed and let go. Paul continued to write as I explained how Jesus did indeed keep His word. I marveled that Daddy did not die alone. And that Jesus had taken care of each one of us very well.

Driving home, I thought about Daddy's lying in the seat of the car that night, waiting for the sheriff's deputy to arrive. Did he pray then? He certainly had time.

I also thought about the months and years following Daddy's death. After Mama was released from jail, I married Grant, moved to another town twelve miles away, and finished high school.

Mama got a job waiting tables at a local truck stop and took another job on the side. Her male and female clientele, on more than one occasion, attempted to molest my brothers and sisters, but the Lord intervened every time. Lori has distinct memories of these occurrences and how Jesus came to her and our siblings' rescue. Every. Time. Sometimes they had to run into the woods behind the house to escape.

Daddy had good reason to be concerned about leaving us, but Jesus was true to His word. Dean is in a mental health institution, where he is well taken care of, and the rest of us have successful lives. All of us are serving the Lord.

I happened to be reading a book with my eighth-grade students titled *Wrapped in Rain* by Charles Martin. In it, Miss Ella Rain says,

"No matter what love goes through or how hard someone tries to kill it, in the end ... love wins."[9]

I totally agree. Love wins! God's love, Jesus's love, Daddy's love. My love.

Love wins. The battle is over.

22

For years, my husband and I have discussed the purchase of a retirement home on a Florida beach. We have visited coastal communities, perused the homes available, and dreamed about the home we may one day purchase. As we get closer to retirement, we talk more and more about our preferences. The type of home we plan to buy has two or more stories. This means there are stairs. I discovered that stairs in a home were still a problem for me. So back to Paul Thompson Counseling I went.

Paul reminded me to tell him everything that I felt, heard, saw, or thought. As soon as we prayed, I closed my eyes and saw the stairs.

I stood at the bottom of the staircase looking up. The top step and landing were bathed in darkness. I felt anxious.

Paul asked, "What would happen if you went up the stairs?"

"I will die, or will have to do stuff I don't want to do."

"Jesus, how do you respond to that?"

I saw a round light about the size of a basketball to the right of the top step. I told Paul, and he asked, "What does that mean to you?"

Before I could answer, Jesus said, *"I'm here."*

I told Paul that Jesus waited at the top of the stairs.

> The anxiety vanished and excitement grew. I wanted to be where Jesus was. I headed up the stairs, my eyes on the light.

The closer I came to it, the larger the light became. Walking into it, I found myself in a large three-story house on the beach. The soothing sounds of waves slapping the shore and far-away seagulls calling spoke peace to me. Standing very still, I looked around.

The house, made of weathered wood and painted white throughout, was uncluttered and modestly furnished. I loved it.

I could not contain my excitement. I felt so unfettered and free. The white cotton dress I wore moved easily around my legs as I ran, laughing and giggling, throughout the house and grounds. The lightweight turquoise scarf tied around my waist flapped in the warm summer breeze. Outside, the warm sand caressed my toes.

I flew back up the weathered steps and around the wrap-around porch. Up a set of stairs, I rounded a corner and stopped in front of a walk-in closet. As I stepped inside, the small room lit up. I went deep into the closet. Every corner lit up. I ran back out and through several bedrooms.

The Light, running with me, called out to me, "I am in every room, every closet, at the bottom and top of every set of stairs. Everywhere, yes, anywhere, you go, I am there. Never again will you be mistreated or made to do things you don't want to do in your house."

What overwhelming joy! In my entire life I had never felt such joy.

Paul asked, "Is the little girl or the adult running through the house?"

"It's the adult running, with the happy little girl inside."

He laughed. I sat there, basking in the moment, while he made notes.

Images begin to pop up. I saw Grandma's face and then the faces of Aunt Rose, my fourth-grade teacher, my tenth-grade best friend, and others. I was confused. Why were these images coming to me now? Seeing them, I felt shame.

Jesus said, *"You lied to all of these people."*

I know, but I thought I'd been forgiven for all of my sins.

"You have. They are written only on the tables of your heart."

Huh?

"You need to forgive yourself."

A thick layer of dust covered the bottom of my box. Only the indentions remained, where each rock had been. I shook the box slightly, and the dust almost choked me. Was each particle something I had done wrong?

I thought of those people, and one by one, I apologized to them as I had done in my mind a hundred times. Finally, I gave up. My heart broke. I would never be able to pay the debt I owed them. Pleading with Him—*Help me*—I felt defeated.

Jesus responded softly, *"Give me the box."* Without hesitation, I handed it to Him. He turned it on its side and hit it twice on His thigh. The thick cloud of dust flew toward the cross. Jesus threw the box in the same direction. All of it disappeared, including my brokenness and shame. He looked at me. His eyes and His smile said it best. *It is finished. All is forgiven.*

During my final visit with Paul, we wrapped up all of the loose ends. The nightmares and daytime anxieties were gone. The tears I couldn't, wouldn't, or weren't allowed to cry as a child had been shed in rivers and filled my well. Love, joy, and peace have been restored to me. I am indeed a new creature.

Lying on my right side in our dark-cherry sleigh bed, my head resting on my folded arm, I notice my half-open nightstand drawer. It's six in the morning, and I am wide awake. Every time I move my feet, the motion-sensor nightlight in the master bathroom comes on briefly, illuminating the doorway and casting a warm glow over the room. Grant sleeps still; the peaceful, steady rhythm of his breathing is music to my ears.

I must not have closed the drawer when I removed my jewelry last night after coming in from a seafood dinner in town. The temperature had been below freezing each night for the last two weeks. We turned down the heater before we left and came home to a chilly house. While Grant readjusted the thermostat, I undressed in a hurry, snatching off my earrings and dropping them into the drawer before switching from jeans and a sweater into microfiber pajamas. Then I hurried to find Grant so I could snuggle into his warmth.

On this winter Saturday morning, I am thankful for my warm husband, home, and microfiber. When I woke, it was too early to even think about getting up, so I lay there, praying the Lord's Prayer over my family, praising Him, and enjoying the peace of mind He has given me.

My feet moved again as I reached over to close the drawer, and in the warm glow, an iridescence caught my eye. I lifted the string of pearls from the drawer before closing it and hold them clustered to my chest. They are not dirty, broken, or in disarray. They are beautiful.

How often I have enjoyed these pearls with no thought of how they came to be. Running my fingers around one pearl, I see it so clearly. Smooth and glossy now, but birthed in pain.

Each of these pearls began as an irritation and source of pain in an oyster. Instinctively, in survival mode, the oyster formed a pearl sac around the intruder and secreted nacre to cover it. Layer upon layer of smoothing nacre coated the problem, making it less irritating and, eventually, painless. In the process, something marvelous and beautiful was formed.

Strung together, these pearls created an image of loveliness, complementing and reflecting each other. When others admire the pearls, the oyster's pain never comes to mind. They only see the beauty of the iridescent nacre.

I see my life as a string of events. Some are good; many, not so much. Each painful past event, after all of the negative emotions and debt were removed, remained an ugly irritation. It happened; I can't pretend it didn't. Every time the irritation is remembered, though, grace reminds me of forgiveness and restoration and lavishes on another smooth layer of peace, layer upon layer, until one day, tranquility completely encapsulates the irritation and silences the pain. Only beauty remains.

Life goes on. God's grace and perfect concept of forgiveness enables each one of us to rise above the suffering and see beauty instead of ashes—a beautiful life here and then eternity in heaven.

The last book of the Bible reveals to us that the gates of heaven, the very entrances into that place of splendor, are each one pearl (Revelation 21:21). Could this aspect of God's heavenly design be significantly more than just a description of its beauty? Is it possible God wants us to be reminded that His iridescent grace, extending forgiveness to all, is the only way in? I think so.

I am not a victim but a victor. And like the oyster, I am a survivor with pearls.

Prayer

> Casting all your care upon him; for he careth for you.
> —1 Peter 5:7

Is there something that continues to cause you emotional pain, especially when you see or think of the person who hurt you? You don't have to continue carrying it. Jesus wants to restore to you what that person took from you when he or she hurt you, but He can't until you give Him the debt. Please, give it to Jesus.

If you continue to carry negative feelings and the debt owed you, it will only hurt you. It does not hurt your offender. Please pray this prayer and unload the burden. It does not excuse what that person did to you; it sets you free from it. If there are multiple hurts by the same person, pray this prayer for each individual hurt. This is necessary because each hurt is different and carries its own debt. The same hurt multiple times can be grouped. (Replace "he" with "she," if needed, as you pray.)

True Lord Jesus, thank You for extending grace to me, forgiving me of my sins. You paid the debt for my sins with Your blood on the cross, and I am eternally grateful.

I have been hurt by _____ when he _____, and I realize I have not forgiven him and cleared the debt.

First, I choose to give You the negative feelings I have regarding this incident (anger, hate, resentment, fear, revenge, sadness, shame, etc.). Please take the _____ away.

Now that the _____ is gone, I realize _____ owes me _____. I know he can never repay this debt. I choose to extend grace to him and forgive him. I give You the debt owed to me and know that as You lay it at the foot of the cross, Your blood pays the debt, and I receive _____ from You. Thank You.

If you prayed this prayer sincerely, you are free from this burden. Every time you see or think of the offender, remember the grace and forgiveness you gave, creating a pearl in place of the former pain.

Endnotes

1. God communicates with us according to our individual gifts, personality traits, and learning styles. In other words, He connects with who we are. He makes conversing with Him as easy as possible for us. I am a visual/auditory learner, so that is how He communicates with me. There are as many combinations of gifts, traits, and styles as there are people. Some people are kinesthetic learners and communicate with God as they are doing an activity. I have a friend who has a wonderful time connecting with God on her morning jogs. Be aware, though, that not every thought that enters your mind is from God. Spending time in prayer and Scripture study will fine-tune your spiritual senses to know whether the communication is truly from God. And Scripture will always support anything truly from Him.
2. W. T. Neilson, Captain, USN, Commanding Officer. Navy Personnel Record of Commendation, 29 September 1949
3. S. A. Hulett, Lt. MC. USNR. Report of Medical Examination, July 1970
4. J. L. Browntree, By direction of CO. Report of Enlisted Performance Evaluation, Oct. 1968
5. CDR. C. A. Saunders, SC, USN. Report of Enlisted Performance Evaluation, Dec. 1969
6. LCDR J. C. Sergent, SC, USN. Report of Enlisted Performance Evaluation, June 1970
7. Matthew 6:12.
8. Warner, Anna B., "Jesus Loves Me." Poem originally published in 1860; music added by W. Bradbury in 1862.
9. Martin, Charles. *Wrapped in Rain* (Nashville: Thomas Nelson, 2005). Used by permission.

CPSIA information can be obtained at www.ICGtesting.com
Printed in the USA
LVOW11s1306040516

486556LV00001B/1/P